JIMMY McMENEMY
Celtic's Napoleon

JIMMY McMENEMY
Celtic's Napoleon

DAVID POTTER

Published in Great Britain in 2012 by The Derby Books Publishing Limited, 3 The Parker Centre, Mansfield Rd, Derby, DE21 4SZ

This paperback edition published in Great Britain in 2013 by DB Publishing a imprint of JMD Media Ltd.

SBN 978-1-78091-155-7

Printed and bound by Copytech (UK) Ltd, Peterborough

CONTENTS

ACKNOWLEDGEMENTS

I have had a great deal of help and encouragement in writing this book. The staff at the Mitchell Library have been very helpful, as have the various Celtic historians like Tom Campbell, Pat Woods, Paul Lunney and George Sheridan whose work I have consulted. On the Partick Thistle side 'Stu The Jag' was very helpful, and for Scotland and Scottish League games, the London Hearts website has been particularly good.

But I am mainly indebted to the late Eugene MacBride whose fascicles on every Celtic game ever played are invaluable. In addition, I'd like to thank the Celtic Graves Society for their superb efforts in keeping alive the traditions of this great club of ours, particularly those who took me to see the grave of Napoleon in Dalbeth Cemetery one miserable rainy day.

The errors and omissions are all mine!

INTRODUCTION

Jimmy McMenemy was one of Celtic and Scotland's truly great players. He played for Celtic for almost twenty years at a time when Celtic were at the top of Scottish and world football, and he was the man that made it all happen for them, generally agreed to be the star of the team that won six League Championships in a row from 1905 until 1910. Little wonder that he earned the nickname at an early stage of his career of Napoleon, for he was the midfield general of that great Celtic side. He also played his part in quite a few triumphs for Scotland, notably against England in 1910 and 1914. Like quite a few others he suffered (indirectly) from the Great War, including a very serious attack of Spanish flu in November 1918 to which he almost succumbed.

Yet he was also a very sporting player, a quiet, unassuming family man whose sons carried on the great McMenemy tradition of playing the game. Arguably his contribution to the Celtic cause as a player was matched by his contribution in the late 1930s as the trainer of the great Celtic side who won the all-British Empire Exhibition Trophy of 1937. Perhaps he was the Napoleon behind that triumph as well! He remains without doubt one of the great characters of early 20th century Scottish football, and his story deserves to be told.

Chapter 1

NAPOLEON

The name 'Napoleon' possibly means less in the early years of the twenty-first century than it did to previous generations. Napoleon was of course the Corsican who emerged from the chaos of the French Revolution of 1789 and the years following to become Emperor of France. Unfortunately, he was unable to abstain from the traditional disastrous French policy of the Kings of previous centuries which involved fighting wars against the British and the Prussians, he undertook the invasion of the massive country called Russia (in winter!) and eventually came to grief at the Battle of Waterloo in 1815.

But he had his great moments. At one point he was the undisputed master of mainland Europe, regularly hammering Austrians, Prussians and anyone else who opposed him and creating in France a system of government that was away in advance of anything else at the time. If only he had not over-reached himself by attacking Russia in winter (always a bad idea, as Hitler would discover as well) and by refusing to come to some sort of agreement with the British (like them or lump them, Great Britain does tend to win more wars than it loses), he would have today been feted as one of the greatest men who ever lived and given pretentious titles like 'the master of modern Europe' and so on.

The British attitude to 'Nap' 'Boney' (his full name was Napoleon Bonaparte) or the 'Corsican' throughout the nineteenth century was ambivalent. To some people, he was the greatest scoundrel who had ever lived, responsible for the deaths of so many people, but he was also much admired. It is easy to admire an enemy when he has been defeated. It is less easy, although by no means uncommon to respect an enemy even when the fighting is still going on. The British, for example, always admired Erwin Rommel, the Desert Fox of the early 1940s, and the ancient Romans had a wee soft spot for Hannibal, the Carthaginian who led them a merry dance for many years, crossed the Alps with elephants and did things like give his name to the modern city of Barcelona (Hannibal's family name was Barca) – all with one eye. Napoleon was like this – admired and respected, and, after he had been defeated, no longer feared or abhorred.

This can perhaps begin to explain why a Scottish footballer, from the safe distance of a century after the floruit of 'Boney' was called 'Napoleon'. It is still difficult to imagine this happening in modern times. Will there ever, for example, be a footballer nicknamed 'Fuhrer' or 'Hitler' or 'Saddam' or 'Bin Laden'? There was of course Franz Beckenbauer who was nicknamed the 'Kaiser', but he was a German and so nicknamed by Germans in the first instance in the 1970s, then accepted by the rest of the world as a welcome sign that the 'Hang The Kaiser' hysteria of the 1920s was now at last beginning to die down – after 50 years!

The name 'Napoleon', of course, still dominated cultural life in Europe for the next hundred years after Waterloo. Jokes like 'What was the name of the Frenchman who stood in front of a cannon?' (answer 'Napoleon Blownapart') were of course common on the Victorian music hall, and there was the serious point that Napoleon's nephew, a well meaning but foolish individual who misguidedly called himself Napoleon III, may well have alienated British support when he picked a fight with Bismarck's Prussians in 1870. Had he not been called 'Napoleon', the British might have come to the help of France (as of course they would do 40 years later in 1914 when France was similarly attacked by the Germans). As it was, the name 'Napoleon' was destroyed in the political sense in the capitulation of France in 1871.

But why was James McMenemy of Celtic and Scotland nicknamed 'Napoleon'? No one really seems to know when it was first applied to him, but given the historical background, one can see a few similarities. Military nicknames were not uncommon – Sandy McMahon had been called 'the Duke' and James McLaren 'the auld general', and frequently we find references in football reports to teams defending like 'the thin red line' and the weather being 'as cold as it had been at Balaclava'. Maybe it was a welcome sign that football was beginning to take over from more warlike activities in people's consciousness.

1914 destroyed such optimism, of course, but before 1914, Celtic had unearthed a great side which dominated Scottish football from the years 1904 to 1910, then after a few years of slightly less achievement, they had risen again to win the Scottish League and Cup Double in 1914. Good players abounded, and indeed one of the great things of that team was that they all played for each other, they were all team players and they would not have tolerated anyone who thought himself better than anyone else. It was no accident for example that the mighty half-back line of Young, Loney and Hay were frequently mentioned as a unit, and the great Jimmy Quinn in the forward line, shy and occasionally socially insecure, was modest to a fault. McMenemy similarly was not the sort of man who thrust himself forward.

Quinn was indeed 'just an ordinary man' (as was frequently said about him) who genuinely did not think that he was anything special. This was true even though all of Great Britain (particularly after his performance for Scotland against England at Hampden in 1910) thought he was the greatest player on earth with even the snobby, middle-class Queen's Park-supporting *The Glasgow Herald* regularly uttering paeans of adulation. The English Press too sincerely sang his praises and sent their reporters regularly to Glasgow to see mundane sounding games like Celtic v St Mirren in order to see the great Jimmy Quinn and the others of this fine side.

It is sometimes however the quieter members of the team who play the most important role. John Clark and Jim Craig, for example, played as important a part at Lisbon as did Billy McNeill and Jimmy Johnstone. Jimmy McMenemy was like this. Sometimes he seemed to be having a quiet game, but the more perspicacious of the supporters and the journalists soon twigged that it was indeed McMenemy who was behind all the moves – the thrusts of Quinn, the rapier attacks of Bennett and the powerful play of Peter Somers and later the phenomenally talented Patsy Gallacher.

McMenemy was also one of the few men who had the ear of Willie Maley, the manager. Maley, in theory the 'match secretary' or 'secretary/manager', rose during the phenomenally successful first 20 years of the 20th century, to become the supremo of Celtic, and was referred to uncompromisingly as 'The Boss'. The trouble with Maley was that he did share a few characteristics of dictators. The first half of the 20th century saw the downfall of many dictators (including eventually in 1940, Maley himself), and much of their demise could be attributed to bullying their underlings and not listening to their advice.

Maley was certainly guilty of all that, but for some reason he would always be careful to listen to McMenemy and his suggestions. On one famous occasion in 1912, McMenemy and he together worked out a solution to a problem, and their successful dealing with this conundrum probably won Celtic four or five League championships. They were a mighty strong combination when working together and both Maley and McMenemy were aware of this when they came together again in the 1930s. But McMenemy was always careful to give the sometimes vainglorious and frequently headstrong Maley his place. McMenemy would seldom claim the credit. He was simply not built like that.

But this is not to say that McMenemy was one of the 'meek' who would 'inherit the earth' as the Beatitudes of the New Testament would have it. Far from it. McMenemy could frequently score a spectacular goal himself, and would be rightly praised for it. But his main strength lay in his leadership. He was not of course the captain. He was too self-effacing to be captain, even though his trademark cry of 'Keep The Heid, Celtic!' was frequently heard.

The honour of being captain belonged to James Hay and later Sunny Jim Young. But the ever-popular McMenemy was the mentor of the forward line, the encourager, the prompter, the string-puller, the man who made things happen, the man who was more than most responsible for Celtic's domination of the footballing world. That was why, perhaps, he was called 'Napoleon'.

And unlike the first Napoleon, Jimmy McMenemy never met his Waterloo.

Chapter 2

EARLY DAYS AND RUTHERGLEN GLENCAIRN

J immy McMenemy was born as James McMenamin at half-past midnight on 11 October 1880 at 146 King Street, Rutherglen. His parents John McMenamin and Hannah O'Dagan (sometimes called Degan, Dagan or even Deacon) had been married on 19 July 1875, and James was not their first child. John is described as a Steel Work Labourer. The confusion over names need not concern us too much. It certainly did not concern Jimmy himself for he was happy to sign himself James McMenamin on all official documents such as the Birth Certificates of his children, but on the football field he was always Jimmy McMenemy – apart of course when he was called Napoleon.

His mother's maiden name was similarly not a real problem. The names given all sounded the same, and we must remember that although Hannah herself was not necessarily illiterate (and even if she was, this was no uncommon phenomenon in Victorian Glasgow), the McMenamins of Rutherglen in 1880 lived in a society which was much less literate than it is now. There would not have been a great many occasions when things had to be written down. John McMenamin, Jimmy's father, was certainly not illiterate, for he signed Jimmy's Birth Certificate.

It was obvious from an early stage that Jimmy was to be a tricky football player, and of course this was the era that everyone was mad on football in Scotland, not least because it was one area of life in which Scotland could beat England. He is reported as having played for a team called Rutherglen Young Celtic, then Cambuslang Bluebell, then Cambuslang Hibs before earning a trial for Dundee, although it has proved impossible to track this down as pseudonyms like 'Smith' 'Brown' and 'McDonald' were used to protect the identity of any youngster.

In 1900 he signed for the up and coming local junior team founded a few years earlier in 1896. They were called Rutherglen Glencairn, a team whose first committee meetings had been held in the old Rutherglen Jail (after it had ceased to be used for imprisonment of offenders!). Their Latin motto was 'Ex fumo fama' – fame comes from smoke, a reference one presumes to the steel forges nearby. They played at a ground called Southcroft Park, a ground which survived for well over 100 years before it was demolished and the Glens were moved to another ground. In the late 1890s, there was a Celtic connection in Colonel Shaughnessy who played a few games for the Glens before becoming a Celtic Director. They were a successful club who won the Glasgow Junior League in 1899.

A year later another boy joined the club, and the two became firm friends. This was a fellow called 'Sandy' Bennett, later to become known as Alec. He played at centre-forward, was a prolific goalscorer and fed off the promptings of McMenemy to launch Glens to previously unheard of levels of glory. Jimmy and Alec talked, ate and slept football – it being far more important than anything else, more important than girls, politics or the Boer War – and were always seen together both on and off the field. There was one point, however, on which they differed. Jimmy being a good Catholic loved the Celtic, whose ground at Parkhead was not too far away, and he went to see them when he was not playing himself, whereas Alec, a non-Catholic, tended to favour the team from the west of the city who had won the Scottish League in 1899, 1900, 1901 and 1902 – the Rangers. It was however a friendly argument between the boys. Unlike many others, they never fell out about it.

1902 was a significant year in British history. There was the horrific Ibrox Disaster in early April when 26 spectators died at the Scotland v. England game, the Boer War came to an end, there was the Coronation of King Edward VII to look forward to and the Australians, with Victor Trumper and Joe Darling on board, were in England to battle for the Ashes. But for the two young men, all these things were of less importance than the great things that were happening for them on the football field. Both were attracting the attention of senior teams, notably Everton and Celtic, but even that took second place to the exploits of Rutherglen Glencairn who in 1902 won the Scottish Junior Cup, the Glasgow Junior League and the Glasgow Exhibition Trophy.

They had already won the Glasgow Junior League by the time that the Scottish Junior Cup Final was played on 10 May 1902. They had reached the Final of this mighty trophy by beating Parkhead, Burnbank Athletic, Glasgow Perthshire and Strathclyde, and the Final against Maryhill was scheduled for Meadowside, the home of Partick

Thistle. A massive crowd turned up to see this Final and huge receipts of £261 17s and 9d were reported, with *The Evening Times* hoping, indeed expecting, that the Scottish Junior Football Association would make a substantial donation to the Ibrox Disaster Fund.

The teams were;

Rutherglen Glencairn: Sinclair: Kinnon and McLean; Brannan, Russell and Williamson: Leitch, McMenemy, Bennett, Underwood and McEwen.

Maryhill: Robertson: Coleman and Walker: Stevenson, Haggerty and Euston; Lily, Queen, Swift, Lang and Sillars.

Referee: Mr. R.T. Murray, Stenhousemuir.

Maryhill, who had more supporters, started well and at one stage were two up before Bennett scored twice to level the score. Curiously, McMenemy is hardly mentioned in reports of the game, other than in the indirect way of 'the forward line was well orchestrated and co-ordinated' – something that would be true of press reports of Jimmy in future years. Willie Maley, Celtic's energetic Manager, for ever on the trail of young talent and who had been watching McMenemy and Bennett for some time, continued to be impressed.

The replay was held two weeks later on 24 May, again at Meadowside. The teams were the same but this time the receipts were £587 and as the admission charge was six old pence, one can work out that the crowd must have been well in excess of 20,000. It was, in fact, a record gate for a junior game. The strong wind was a factor. Glencairn played with the wind in the first half, and McMenemy scored an easy tap-in when Robertson dropped a McEwen cross towards the end of the first half, but like the rest of the team when Maryhill piled on the pressure, McMenemy was compelled to defend in the second half. The Press are full of praise for the Rutherglen team. McMenemy is, once again, not singled out for glory but the comment is made of the forward line, 'Individually and collectively, this division was a perfect one'.

Thus Jimmy had won a Scottish Junior Cup medal. He and his family were proud of all this, but even better was to come, and that was when, on the Sunday or the Monday immediately after the replay, Maley offered him terms to sign for Celtic. He allegedly signed 'up a close in Union Street', presumably on Monday 26 May 1902. We know this because on that night, Rutherglen Glencairn were playing a friendly against Saturday's opponents, Maryhill with the proceeds all to go to the Ibrox Disaster Fund. McMenemy could not play in this game (which Glens lost 0–2) because he had now signed on the dotted line for Maley's Celtic.

This club had now been playing football for fourteen years, one of the newer teams, but they had already won the Scottish Cup three times and the Scottish League four times. More significant than that was their massive impressive new stadium, the envy of most of the British Isles, and the uncompromising support that they enjoyed from the community they had been formed to represent – the Glasgow Irish.

Chapter 3

CELTIC AND THE GREAT DAYS 1902–1910

When McMenemy put pen to paper for Celtic on 26 May 1902, he was not yet 22 years old. Some may well have thought that he had joined the wrong team, for 1902 had not been a great season for the Celtic club. Indeed it had not been a great season for Scottish football, reeling as it still was from the effects of the horrendous Ibrox Disaster of 5 April of that year – something that shook Scotland and caused letters to appear in newspapers suggesting that football was the work of the devil and should be banned. That was of course from the lunatic fringe of religious extremists, but quite a few people inside football were questioning the wisdom of allowing such large crowds to gather at stadia which were struggling to cope with them.

Celtic had few problems with their stadium but on the playing field, they were somewhat in the doldrums. They had not won the

Scottish League since 1898, and there was a certain belief that hegemony was passing, perhaps permanently, to Rangers on the other side of the city who had indeed won the Scottish League for four seasons in a row. Celtic had won the Scottish Cup in 1899 and 1900, but had lost the last two finals – bad luck and goalkeeping errors playing a part in the 1901 3–4 reverse to Hearts, and a somewhat indifferent performance in the 1902 Cup Final seeing them lose the Scottish Cup to the team that some still regarded as their mother club – the Hibernians of Edinburgh. This game had had to be played at Celtic Park, for it was only three weeks after the Ibrox Disaster, and therefore Ibrox was still out of action whereas the massive new stadium that was to be built for Queen's Park was still at an embryonic stage and would not be opened for more than a year.

Celtic's poor form of the last few years (pessimists were predicting a permanent eclipse and even extinction in spite of the obvious assets of a large ground and a huge support) meant that the enthusiastic young Manager Willie Maley was permanently scouring the British Isles for men that were fit to wear the Celtic colours. Maley's dynamism did of course have an adverse effect on his marriage and family life, but he would never regret what he did for the institution that he was happy to call his 'obsession'. He travelled the length and breadth of the country looking for new talent, and his natural geniality and sociability meant that he built up a large network of contacts who would tip him off if a good young player became available.

He did not have far to go for Jimmy McMenemy. McMenemy was playing for a team called the Cambuslang Hibs when he was given his first trial for Celtic. This was in August 1900 in a pre-season trial in a game against Motherwell which Celtic lost. Although Maley was impressed by the trickery of the slender youngster, he possibly felt that he was not yet big enough or tough enough to shield himself from the robust tackling that would undeniably come his way in the hard school that was the Scottish League. Dundee who had given him a trial a year earlier seemed to have come to a similar conclusion.

But McMenemy kept playing successfully for Rutherglen Glencairn, and optimistic noises kept coming to Maley's ears about the tricky young player who could pass well, had a tremendous shot and had, in spite of his apparently frail physique, the energy and stamina to last ninety minutes. Indeed he was the man mainly responsible for the phenomenal success that the Glens had enjoyed that year. Maley decided that it was time to have another look.

In one of the games that had been arranged with commendable speed for the Ibrox Disaster Fund, Celtic took on Blackburn Rovers at Parkhead on Wednesday 16 April. McMenemy played for the club then, although under the pseudonym of 'Smith'. (There was nothing necessarily sinister about this ploy – future Celt Davie Hamilton also played in that game under the pseudonym of 'Wilson' – for it was common practice at the time and seems to have its origins in nothing other than a desire to shield the player from the unwelcome attentions of rival clubs.) 3,000 fans saw a 'promising display' from the youngster in an otherwise dull 0–0 draw.

He played again at Parkhead on Monday 28 April – but this time for the opposition! Teams other than Celtic had been impressed by the excellent form of Rutherglen Glencairn in 1902, not least Everton who had come second in the English League, but the imminent Coronation of King Edward VII was not without significance in McMenemy getting a trial for Everton at Parkhead. This was because a tournament had been arranged between the top two teams in both England and Scotland viz. Celtic, Rangers, Everton and Sunderland, with Rangers generously putting up a trophy which they had won last year at the Glasgow Exhibition for the winners. It was to be called the British League Cup or the Coronation Cup, but historians had tended to go for the former because the Coronation Cup is usually reckoned to be the more famous one of 1953.

The draw put English Champions Sunderland to Celtic Park and Rangers the Scottish Champions to Goodison on 30 April and 1 May respectively. But a friendly had already been arranged months previously between Everton and Celtic at Parkhead on Monday 28. Because of the imminence of the British League Cup ties, both teams agreed to play weakened sides and Everton used the opportunity to try out four Rutherglen Glencairn youngsters, one of them being Jimmy McMenemy. A low crowd (Celtic's fans and players were still reeling from their Scottish Cup Final defeat by Hibs two days previously) of about 2,000 saw a sterile 1–1 draw, but Maley saw enough of McMenemy to make a move for him, once Rutherglen's triumphant season was over.

In any case, with Glencairn in the Junior Cup Final, it would give Maley an excellent opportunity to watch McMenemy in a big game. He knew that Glencairn were a good side, for they had already won the Glasgow Junior League, but he needed to see McMenemy under pressure in an important game with a large crowd in attendance. McMenemy, for his own part, had been given more than a nod and a wink that Celtic were interested in him.

Everton may also have expressed an interest, but McMenemy, a home loving Glaswegian with more than a small soft spot for the green and white vertical stripes of 'the Celtic' did not take long to decide who he wanted to play for. In May 1902, McMenemy's long and loving association with Celtic began when he signed 'up a close in Union Street' as tradition had it. It was a difficult time for Celtic, for they had just lost the Glasgow Charity Cup Final to Hibs (the

Glasgow Charity Cup had been expanded this season to include teams like Hibs because of the Ibrox Disaster and the need to make a substantial donation to the Fund) and this time it was a substantial 2–6 beating.

But there was still a little balm in Gilead. The British League Cup Final held on the ridiculously late date of 17 June so as to be as near as possible to the Coronation which was scheduled for 26 June, saw Jimmy Quinn score a hat-trick as Celtic beat Rangers 3–2. McMenemy watched this game as a Celtic player, and this game duly passed into Parkhead folklore. Ironically the Coronation had to be postponed until August when the King was diagnosed with a rare form of appendicitis, called perityphlitis. This was in 1902 a dangerous and often fatal condition, and needed a difficult operation in which the surgeons were in uncharted waters. Prayers were said in Churches throughout the Empire for the 60-year-old roué who was to inherit the throne after several decades of being the Prince of Wales. He did survive, was crowned in August and remained King until his death in 1910. His reign saw a great Celtic side, and this is why McMenemy's time is often referred to as the Edwardian Celts.

At the start of the 1902–03 season, the young McMenemy, not yet 22, was wise enough to realise that he would not just walk into the Celtic team, for the standard and expectations were a great deal higher than at junior level. He was content to bide his time, playing in the occasional benefit or tour game for the first team when he was not turning out for the 'stiffs' or the 'ham and eggers' as the reserve team was called, the latter name coming from the fact that not all the reserves were paid, but they were given their tea at a restaurant or hotel after the game. He was also given the occasional game for East Stirlingshire and Stenhousemuir. Maley had an arrangement with both these teams and liked to blood his youngsters there, for they were sufficiently far out of Glasgow to keep them away from the prying eyes of Rangers and Queen's Park, but not too far away that he himself couldn't turn up unexpectedly to observe their progress.

But on Monday 29 September 1902, (the Edinburgh autumn holiday) Jimmy made his first-team debut. It was against Hearts at Tynecastle, and it was thanks to an injury to Tommy McDermott sustained in the 1–0 win against Third Lanark on the Saturday, that McMenemy was given his chance at inside-left. He is neither raved about nor criticised in reports, but the team did well enough, earning a 2–2 draw with Peter Somers grabbing a late equaliser with virtually the last kick of the ball.

McDermott, another friend of Jimmy's from Rutherglen and a fine footballer whose Achilles heel was his attitude and reluctance to bow to the sometimes tyrannical Maley, returned after that, but the form of the team continued to be unpredictable. They reached the Glasgow Cup Final for example but collapsed distressingly to Third Lanark in a 0–3 defeat not entirely explained by Willie Orr's absence because he missed his train! McMenemy might well have been justified in feeling that Celtic might have done better with him in the team.

McMenemy was next given a game at inside-right on 22 November against a now defunct club called Port Glasgow Athletic. It was his first home game, and it was one of these days on which one wonders why football ever became popular in Scotland. Dark, wet and windy, it was November at its worst. The attendance was described as 'poor', which possibly means as few as 3,000, and the pitch was so wet that Celtic had to change strips at half-time. Unfortunately they did not seem to have another set of the green and white vertical stripes, so had to come out in an all green jersey.

It was a game in which McMenemy impressed with a few deft touches, eliciting the occasional round of applause, but the crowd were beginning to get impatient by Celtic's inability to score and to convert their overall superiority into goals. Eventually Willie Loney playing as attacking centre-half managed to score half way through the second half. Darkness was falling fast when Davie Hamilton scored from a McMenemy pass, and it was virtually dark when McMenemy himself scored in the crepuscular gloom at full-time to earn a smile from men that he admired, Johnny Campbell who was playing inside-left that day, Jimmy Quinn, Willie Loney and of course Manager Maley himself.

McMenemy was given a run in the team after that, but then was duly returned to the reserves. The youngster had given Maley and the Celtic Board enough to make them think that he was worth persevering with. He had good ball control, could pass well, had a turn of speed but was slight in build and needed to build up strength in his shoulders to ward off hefty tackles from defenders. He was told to train hard and he would be given another chance, perhaps in the spring when the weather improved.

In his absence, Celtic's League challenge faltered (Hibs would win the Championship that year) and in the Scottish Cup they collapsed ignominiously in the quarter-final to Rangers. McMenemy suffered from the bad winter in that very few games were played, but he kept his head down at Parkhead, listened and learned. He was given a game at Clune Park in the return match against Port Glasgow (and scored Celtic's only goal), then played a few games in the low-profile Inter-City League before earning his spurs properly in the Glasgow Charity Cup, in which he won his first medal, as things began to stir at Celtic Park.

Spring 1903 was the morning star of the greatest side ever to play football. Not only was McMenemy given a run at inside-left, but two other men were brought it. One was McMenemy's friend from Glencairn, Alec Bennett a man who could play in the centre-forward position or on the right wing, and McMenemy was instrumental in bringing him to Parkhead. And it all happened on a train between Edinburgh and Glasgow.

It was a Monday Holiday, 20 April, and Celtic were at Tynecastle for a meaningless Inter City League game against Hearts. Celtic fielded virtually a reserve team, and Hearts had a few trialists as well, one of them a trialist called 'Johnston'. 'Johnston' was none other than Alec Bennett, who had indeed travelled through on the same train from Glasgow as Celtic, and he scored in the 3–0 Hearts victory. Maley of course recognised him, and told McMenemy to 'have a word' with Alec.

On the train home, Jimmy sat beside him in a separate compartment, and told him that Maley wanted to offer him terms for next season. Bennett was of course flattered but there were two objections – one was that he remained a Rangers supporter and was hoping for an offer for them, and the other was that Hearts had actually offered him a contract at full time, which he said he would consider. But such was the persuasive talent of McMenemy that Bennett appeared at Celtic Park the following day and signed for Celtic – but only on condition that he could leave if a good offer came his way. It was a great decision for both Celtic and Bennett, and McMenemy's part in all this did not go unnoticed by Willie Maley.

The other great signing was a fair-haired Ayrshireman who had become homesick at Bristol Rovers. He was played at centre-half for the meantime, and his name was James Young. Neither of these two, Young or Bennett was a Celt in the ethnic sense of the word – indeed Bennett, as we have discovered, was an unashamed lover of Rangers – but what a difference these two made! It was perhaps a deliberate ploy by Maley to prevent Celtic from becoming over-dependent on their own indigenous Catholic support. Football was continuing to expand, and Celtic must develop with it, Maley being very conscious that the name 'Celtic' must include both Scotland and Ireland.

After a tough 0–0 draw against Hibs in the Charity Cup semi-final (Hibs and other non-Glasgow teams being included once again to boost the Ibrox Disaster Fund), McMenemy turned it on in the replay in the inside-left position, constantly supplying Bennett in the centre and Quinn on the left wing. Quinn rampaged down the left wing, cut inside at will, and scored four goals. McMenemy, whom discerning supporters recognised as the brains behind it all, scored the other as Hibs, the League Champions were beaten 0–5.

A song was born that night as gloating Celtic fans with a particular spite at the Edinbugh Irishmen sang:

'Oh dear, what can the matter be?
Hibs got beat at Cathkin last Thursday
Four goals from Quinn and one from McMenemy
Oh what fun it was there!'

This song was much altered in future years to include references to Rangers, but it had its genesis that night, and such was the renewed enthusiasm in the Celtic community that 15,000 (a huge crowd for the Glasgow Charity Cup) turned up at Cathkin on the Saturday for the Final. Long queues at the turnstiles (or 'payboxes' as they were called) caused a delay, but it was worth waiting for, as Bennett scored a hat-trick this time and Quinn and Loney the other goals in the 5–2 defeat of St.Mirren. The creative and thoughtful McMenemy now had his first medal, the first of a phenomenal amount – and a first team spot would be his for the next 17 years!

That this was a new and young Celtic team was made obvious in the first game of the 1903–04 season when a new strip was unveiled.

The colours were still green and white, but this time they were horizontal rather than vertical. They were still called 'stripes' – the introduction of the word 'hoops' came almost a century later – and they did somehow add to the impression that Celtic were young, fast and fit. Indeed they were, and McMenemy fitted well into this side.

But success did not come instantly. Maley kept experimenting with the side trying to find the best combination of the talent that definitely existed, and the mighty side assembled only gradually. The half-back line of Young, Loney and Hay, for example, was played together by accident following a spate of injuries at Airdrie in early January and only properly came together a month later during a prolonged struggle to beat Dundee in the Scottish Cup. Jimmy Quinn would eventually settle at centre-forward, fortunately in time for the Scottish Cup Final in April, but Maley took little time to be convinced of one thing, and that was that he had a star inside-forward in Jimmy McMenemy.

He was a level-headed youngster as well with an ability to get on with everyone – an important asset in a football team, for Maley knew from his dealings with the wild elements like Doyle and McKeown how easily trouble could arise – and McMenemy could 'read' a game in the sense that he knew which of his own players was having a good game and which of the opposition was having a poor game. He could score goals, as well. And perhaps his strongest point was his ability to accept that he had had a bad game, and to bounce back from it. He had a shocker, for example, in the first ever game played at Hampden Park on 31 October 1903 – a bad-tempered affair which Queen's Park won 1–0 – and had to be dropped for the next game, but he took it on the chin and came roaring back.

But the team of the 1903–04 season was Third Lanark. With ex-Celt Johnny Campbell in the side and managed by a man with the unlikely name of Frank Heaven, Thirds would win the Scottish League (for the first and only time in their history) beating Celtic twice in the early part of the season, and in the Glasgow Cup. The Glasgow Cup Final was played on 21 November 1903 at Ibrox, and Celtic were indebted to McMenemy for a late equaliser after many of the 20,000 crowd had decided they were going home. Sadly, Jimmy could not repeat his heroics the following week in the replay, and this time Third Lanark survived the late Celtic barrage and won the prestigious Glasgow Cup.

Celtic would get their revenge however in the Scottish Cup semi-final at Parkhead (neutral venues for semi-finals was still almost a decade away) on 19 March 1904 when late goals by Jimmy Quinn and Bobby Muir saw Celtic through to a 2–1 victory. 36,000 was a large crowd for 1904, and they were treated to a tremendous Celtic display (hinting at great things to come) in the second half after a first half that was described as 'indifferent' or 'mediocre'. Two men were singled out – one was James Young, already commonly referred to as 'Sunny Jim' as he would now be for the rest of his life, and the other was Jamie (sic) McMenemy. The *Glasgow Observer* chortles that 'Young supplied the power, the thrust and the drive, McMenemy the trickery and the wizardry'.

This brought Celtic to their fifth Scottish Cup Final in six years, and it was against the team from the west of the city who had won four League Championships in a row but who, in spite of winning the Scottish Cup of 1903, gave signs of having faded in the last couple of seasons. This was the Rangers team, possibly the only team that could rival Celtic in terms of support. But they had never really regained their prestige lost in the horrible Ibrox disaster of 1902, the event that would haunt Edwardian football, and Rangers for a long time after that.

As Celtic approached this first Final to be played at the new Hampden ground, a problem developed and it concerned Jimmy's old friend from Rutherglen, Alec Bennett. Alec was a fine centre-forward (although some people felt that he might be a better right winger where he could use his speed and avoid some of the brutal tackles that came the way of centre-forwards) but he had a problem at Celtic Park. Being a non-Catholic, the sensitive Bennett occasionally found some of the cries from the crowd difficult to cope with, and he also had many friends at Ibrox. Unofficial suggestions came to Bennett's ears that he would be welcome there next season.

McMenemy was of course very aware of all this, and did all he could to keep Bennett happy at Parkhead. He even consulted Maley about it (Maley was far more approachable in 1904 than he would be in later life) and McMenemy was possibly distressed to hear that Maley was going to drop Bennett for the imminent Scottish Cup Final, on the grounds that it would be unfair to Bennett. Maley had tactical reasons for this as well, for he had decided that Jimmy Quinn should play in the centre and use his weight to deal with the coarse Rangers defenders. He also wanted to keep Bobby Muir on the right wing, where Bennett might also have played.

For public consumption, Bennett had 'flu' and one wonders what his emotions were when the 1904 Scottish Cup Final became the most famous of them all so far. Celtic were two down, but equalised twice before half-time through Jimmy Quinn and then the same man scored the winner in the second half. It would become known as Quinn's Cup Final, but the modest Jimmy Quinn would always pay tribute to the rest of the team, not least the slender figure of Jimmy McMenemy who supplied most of the ammunition. McMenemy now had his first Scottish Cup medal – he would eventually win seven – and life must have looked good for him, as he was now one of the very few men to possess a Scottish Cup medal and a Scottish Junior Cup medal.

He would also use his diplomatic skills to persuade Alec Bennett to stay at Celtic for the next four years, and what a mighty four years that would be, as 'Bennett, McMenemy, Quinn, Somers and Hamilton' would become one of the great forward lines of Scottish football. It was said at the time that for the average Celtic fan blessed to have seen Willie Maley's incredible team in action, 'there rolled off his tongue trippingly and lovingly a litany that made music for him in five sweet symphonies – Bennett, McMenemy, Quinn, Somers and Hamilton.'

In summer 1904, after a brutal Glasgow Charity Cup Final in which revenge was meted out to poor Jimmy Quinn by a vindictive Rangers defender, the team went on a close season tour of Centre Europe. This must have been a great experience for the young McMenemy to play in Vienna and Prague. The football was crude, in every sense of the word, but Celtic were great ambassadors for Scotland and for the game of football which Manager Maley honestly believed that Celtic had a 'missionary' role in spreading. They were welcomed wherever they went.

The 1904–05 season was, of course, the first of Celtic's six League titles in a row, but for McMenemy it was marred by a bad injury. This occurred at Broomfield, Airdrie on 29 November 1904 at the end of a game that Celtic were winning comfortably, McMenemy having scored twice when he was tackled by Davie Rombach, Airdrie's left-back. McMenemy was carried off while Rombach was spoken to by the referee and was booed everytime he touched the ball thereafter.

It was indeed a shame, for McMenemy had been very impressive in every game he had played that season. It had already included a Glasgow Cup triumph over Rangers in which McMenemy had been instrumental in Bennett's two goals. McMenemy's popularity was growing among the Celtic fans, and his absence would be sorely felt. In fact he missed all of December and January during which time Celtic lost twice, once to Airdrie and once to Dundee, thus imperilling their championship challenge.

But he returned to a great cheer on 4 February 1905 against Morton, and such was his play during the months of February and March that he was awarded a Scottish cap against Ireland on 18 March. This was a great moment for McMenemy, but it was perhaps not as monumental an occasion as it sounded. It was against Ireland, and it was played at Celtic Park where Scotland v Ireland games often were, and to attract a big crowd, no fewer than five Celtic players were invited to play for Scotland. Scotland won 4–0 and reports on McMenemy were favourable, although he was played, eccentrically, on the right wing to allow the prodigious Bobby Walker of Hearts to play at inside-right.

He was not picked for the England game at the Crystal Palace, but his moment would come. Of more immediate concern were the events of 25 March when Celtic went out of the Scottish Cup at the Semi-Final stage to Rangers at Parkhead. Jimmy Quinn was sent off (unfairly), and some misguided individuals invaded the park. It was a lesson to McMenemy of how dangerous passions could be in the game of football. But if Celtic were disappointed by this result, compensation came their way in early May.

Celtic and Rangers finished level at the top of the Scottish League on points, and the authorities decided to have a play-off, using an arranged Glasgow League game between Celtic and Rangers for the purpose. The Glasgow League usually attracted few spectators and was little loved by the fans, but when this one was decreed as the Scottish League decider, it was moved to Hampden and 30,000 appeared to see McMenemy score Celtic's second goal in the 2–1 win which had the supporters 'dancing on the cinders' ie of the terracing. As is often the case, it was a scrappy goal which had important consequences. It was a miskick!

Icing was then added to the cake when the Glasgow Charity Cup was also won at the end of May with McMenemy scoring in both the semi-final and the Final, and clearly now part of a team that was really beginning to impress with frequent references to 'Maley's young side' and 'the green and white brigade', as newspaper reporters began to warm to the excellent football which came out of Parkhead.

Celtic had thus won three honours out of four in the 1904–05 season. Third Lanark had won the Scottish Cup, beating Rangers in the Final. No team had as yet won a Double of the Scottish League and the Scottish Cup in the same season in the same way as Aston Villa and Preston had done in England. It was a target that Celtic would now be aiming for.

But in the summer of 1905, an important thing happened for Jimmy. On 4 July at the Catholic Chapel in Rutherglen, Jimmy married the girl he had been going out with for some time, Rose McCluskey. Rose lived a few doors down from him in Mitchell Street and is described as a French Polisher on the wedding certificate. She was 22 and the daughter of a widow called Maggie McCluskey whose husband James had been a Steel Worker before his death. This turned out to be a successful marriage, producing as it did three boys – John, Frank and Harry who all played professional football – as well as other children, and the marriage lasted 54 years before Rose passed away in September 1959. They would settle at 18 Greenhill Road before moving to McDonald Street (both in Rutherglen), but by 1910 the McMenemys were living almost next door to Celtic Park at 288 Dalmarnock Street.

Celtic didn't quite achieve the Double in season 1905–06 but this was the season that really made Scotland sit up and take notice of what a great side Celtic were with a great run following a defeat on 11 November 1905 (significantly, McMenemy was out injured that day) until 3 February 1906 in which they won 12 League games, scoring 36 goals and conceding four. It was the time when the great forward line of Bennett, McMenemy, Quinn, Somers and Hamilton took off with Quinn scoring the goals, but the ammunition being supplied by the wily McMenemy and Somers. It was also the season that we find the first reference to 'Napoleon' a propos of a game against Airdrie at Celtic Park on 30 September. It was a close game, as often happened when Airdrie were the visitors and the score was 1–1 until the 75th minute but 'when Napoleon scored, a yell of triumph burst from 20,000 throats and the roaring was maintained and grew in volume on to the close'.

The following week Quinn, Somers and McMenemy all scored as Celtic beat Third Lanark in the Final of the Glasgow Cup. This time the crowd was only 20,000 because of incessant heavy rain and the fact that Hampden, big and vast as it was, provided only minimal shelter for rich spectators who could afford to go to the Stand, and none at all for the poorer ones. The Scottish League was won with several games in hand in the month of March 1906, a couple of weeks after a serious disappointment had been sustained in the 1–2 loss to Hearts in the Scottish Cup before well over 50,000 spectators at Celtic Park. The pitch was hard and heavily sanded, something that perhaps militated against Celtic's ball players, and Celtic were without the inspirational Sunny Jim Young. Although McMenemy scored first for Celtic, Hearts' strong team scored twice in the second half and Celtic's hopes of the elusive 'double' were smashed.

It was a matter of some concern that McMenemy was not awarded a Scottish cap again this season, or even a Scottish League cap. His play was certainly good enough, according to the newspapers of the time, but perhaps his slight physique and shy, retiring demeanour counted against him. In addition, it must be said that the competition was strong for the inside-right position with Sandy McFarlane of Dundee, Bobby Walker of Hearts and Jimmy Howie of Newcastle United all in contention – and all playing well for Scotland, when given their opportunity, with Bobby Walker in particular generally reckoned to be close to the best in the world, and earning nicknames like 'the wizard', 'Houdini' and 'the bobby dazzler'.

The end of the season was disappointing for Jimmy, because a defeat from Rangers in the Glasgow Charity Cup was followed by a bad injury at, of all places, the ground of Forres Mechanics on Celtic's tour of the Highlands. This meant that he was left behind on the tour of Europe later that summer. One suspects that McMenemy was not too disappointed to miss out on this tour, for although he had enjoyed everything about the previous one in 1904, he was tired and needed a break from football. He possibly reckoned that if you are to be injured, then summer is by no means that worst time.

Great things beckoned in 1906–07 and even greater in 1907–08. In the former season the team won everything except the Glasgow Charity Cup (the first ever Scottish 'double' of League and Cup in the same season by any team) and in the latter they won everything they entered for, thus becoming without any shadow of doubt the greatest team on earth and enriching the cultural lives of their supporters to an almost unbelievable extent. The 1908 side is compared with the 1967 team which won the European Cup.

Those lucky enough to have seen both were very few (one would have to been mature enough to watch football in 1908, lucky enough to survive war, depression and war again – and still be sufficiently compos mentis et corporis in 1967) generally refused to commit themselves as to who was the better, but the very fact that both teams were mentioned in the same breath is a compliment indeed. It means, for example, that Napoleon was as good as someone like Bobby Murdoch or Bertie Auld. Frankly, that says it all.

A curious thing happened at the start of the 1906–07 season. Goalkeeper Davie Adams was playing in a testimonial game at Ibrox at the start of the season when he cut his palm on a nail sticking out of a goalpost. Ever the chivalrous gentlemen in these days, Rangers felt duty bound to offer Celtic the services of their reserve goalkeeper Tommy Sinclair, a man well known to McMenemy and Bennett for he had played with them for Rutherglen Glencairn in their triumph of 1902. Tommy played nine games for Celtic at the start of the season, eight of which were shut-outs, and even in the game where he conceded two goals (and how angry he was at himself and his team mates!) he had enough to be happy about, for it was the Glasgow Cup Final against Third Lanark which Celtic won 3–2!

Thus Tommy left Parkhead with a Glasgow Cup winners' medal when Davie Adams came back, returned to Ibrox where he still could not hold down a regular spot and was eventually transferred to Newcastle United for whom he played three games (conceding only one goal) as they won the English League that season! He thus has the distinction of playing for both the Scottish and the English League winners in the one season – but sadly without having played in enough games to qualify for a medal in either!

McMenemy's part in Celtic's success in 1907 and 1908 was paramount. He had now developed into a ball winner of some repute, never shirking the tackle, although he was always the first to admit that he was never a great tackler himself – that was the province of

Sunny Jim or Dun Hay – but it was as a purveyor, a carrier of the ball, an evader of tackles, and a passer to the ever ready Jimmy Quinn or Alec Bennett that he became famous. And he could score the occasional goal himself, sometimes at crucial moments like the Scottish Cup semi-final of 1908 at Pittodrie in a goalmouth scrimmage in the 89th minute to deny Aberdeen a chance of a replay. In the Scottish Cup Final of that year, a 5–0 romp over an outclassed St.Mirren, McMenemy was the only forward NOT to score, but it was he who made all the five goals for the others!

Still, International recognition was slow in coming. One could not really claim any sort of anti-Celtic bias (although many did at the time) because other Celtic players, notably Jimmy Quinn were recognised, but it was a source of amazement that the man who made this superb Celtic side tick (McMenemy 'put the tic in Celtic' it was claimed) was not given a chance to perform on the International stage. Those who travelled to Newcastle in 1907, for example, to see a sterile draw between Scotland and England came back convinced that some of the craft of Jimmy McMenemy might have made a difference, especially if he could have had Jimmy Quinn to provide the ammunition for.

A couple of weeks after that International came the Scottish Cup Final of 1907 between Celtic and Hearts and the newspapers said that it would be a great opportunity for fans to decide who was the better inside-right – Bobby Walker or Jimmy McMenemy. Celtic won 3–0, (to the consternation of the massive Hearts support which had travelled from Waverley and Haymarket in 'football specials') and McMenemy was outstanding.

It remained true however that this Celtic team did not really have an outstanding individual. Quinn was famous of course but he was the goalscorer and automatically attracted attention, but the half-

Jimmy McMenemy fourth from left in the middle row of the record breaking Celtic team of 1907–08.

back line of Young, Loney and Hay was a unit who worked together and was strong enough to cope with the one of their number missing. When Willie Loney broke his arm for example or when Jimmy 'Dun' Hay had to have an operation for appendicitis, there was enough cover in the shape of the multi-purpose man from Stenhousemuir, the immortal Alec McNair. In the forward line, Jimmy Quinn missed the Final of the Glasgow Cup of October 1907, but his deputy Davie McLean scored a tremendous pile-driver of a goal.

And the forward line was also a unit, but the difference here was that they all knew each other and they could interchange at will. Bennett for example had been a centre-forward and Jimmy Quinn a left-winger, McMenemy could play in either inside position as could the mercurial comedian called Peter Somers (who entertained the other players when they were away from home) and even the least well known of the quintette, Davie Hamilton, 'the Dancer' could suddenly appear on the other wing or in the centre. This was even more so when Hamilton temporarily lost his place to Bobby Templeton the extrovert who inadvertently caused the Ibrox Disaster of 1902 when a charge down the wing caused the crowd to lean forward simultaneously, and who on another occasion when playing for Kilmarnock, for a dare, walked into a lion's cage at a menagerie!

This ability of these five forwards to read each other and to interchange positions at will and at speed meant that marking them was very difficult for the opposition, and it was a lesson that McMenemy would remember all his life. 'The beauty of the movements of McMenemy, Quinn and Somers is unsurpassed in football' was the opinion of the writer in *The Glasgow Herald*.

The outside world was changing as well, and there were real grounds for optimism. The Prime Minister since late 1905 was a benign Glaswegian called Henry Campbell Bannerman who was at least making some sort of attempt to improve living and social conditions. There was a long way to go, of course, but a vigorous government which contained three future Prime Ministers in Asquith, Lloyd George and Churchill, was determined that the worst excesses of a hundred years industrial growth – things like bubonic plague which surfaced from time to time in the slums of Glasgow – should be tackled. Poor school children could now get a free hot meal at dinner time, for example – a poignant issue for Celtic fans, for was not this the reason for the formation of the club? Campbell Bannerman died in April 1908, and was replaced by Herbert Asquith.

If 1908 was the apogee of this great Celtic side, the next two years represented a decline, but only a slight one. 1908–09 was a remarkable season. Sadly it is remembered for the wrong reasons of the riot at the Scottish Cup Final. This is a shame, for it tends to obscure what happened next in that Celtic played off their backlog of fixtures and by playing eight games in twelve days managed to come from behind to win the Scottish League.

But a lot more happened than that in this season. In the first place the famous right wing pair of Bennett and McMenemy broke up, as Jimmy was this time unable to dissuade Alec from going to Rangers. It will be remembered that Alec wanted to go to Ibrox in 1904 but remained at Celtic. This time, possibly feeling that he had been a part of the 1908 team which won everything, there was not much further he could go with Celtic, Bennett went to Rangers, as he was entitled to do according to the contract he had signed in 1903.

Bennett played better football for Celtic than he did for Rangers, (hardly surprising for Rangers possessed no McMenemy to supply the ammunition!) and it would certainly appear that he was taking a chance, but he ended up with three League medals for Rangers to go with his four for Celtic. Celtic made a few half-hearted complaints about him being 'tapped' by Rangers, but they knew they could not stop him, and it may all have come down to the simple fact that Rangers offered him more money, and as Alec was thinking of marrying his girlfriend Annie Drennen, finance had assumed new importance for 'the artful dodger', as Bennett became known.

Curiously Alec does not seem to have been as vilified by the support as Maurice Johnstone and Kenny Miller in more recent times have (deservedly) been. Indeed, he is looked upon as one of the best outside-rights that Celtic have had and when one thinks that that includes men like Jimmy Delaney and Jimmy Johnstone, that is no mean feat. In addition, he and McMenemy remained friends and indeed teamed up with each other again at International level. It was always said, though, that he was never the same player again after he left Parkhead. He won League medals with Rangers, but never showed the panache that he revealed for Celtic. After the Great War, he became the Manager of Third Lanark.

McMenemy thus had to adjust to the problem of having a new right wing partner. With respect to Dan Munro, Michael Moran and Willie Kivlichan, Bennett was badly missed, but given the general stability of the rest of the team, League form was acceptable after a couple of early defeats to Dundee and St.Mirren.

It was the Glasgow Cup in the autumn of 1908 that caused a certain amount of stir and had its effect on the awful events of April 1909. The problem was draws. Even today, any draw in a Cup-tie will lead to a certain amount of eyebrow raising on the grounds that a replay does not do the coffers of either club any harm. It was particularly tactless therefore when in the Glasgow Cup of autumn 1908, Celtic drew with Queen's Park before beating them, drew with Rangers before beating them and then in the Final against Third Lanark drew twice with them on successive Saturdays in late October.

Feeling now that enough Saturdays had been used up, the Scottish League began to complain. It was normally felt that the Glasgow Cup being an older tournament than the Scottish League should have precedence, but this was pushing things rather far, and the third game was scheduled for Wednesday 28 October 1908.

What happened that day can never be proven, but in front of a far smaller crowd than would have turned up on a Saturday (it was an afternoon kick-off, of course, and in 1908 the idea of 'throwing a sickie' was a dangerous ploy), Celtic conceded an early goal and then collapsed to a 0–4 defeat. This result caused as much of a sensation in 1908 as Partick Thistle's League Cup triumph did in 1971, and Celtic fans were mystified by the half-hearted performances of some of their players. Naturally, rumours spread.

It is of course very easy to jump to conclusions about corruption and match-fixing, but there exist other possible explanations. Alec Bennett was sadly missed; Davie Hamilton, the left-winger was badly injured in the first half and was only a passenger thereafter; Thirds were a good side and may simply have played above themselves while Celtic may have had too many players off form. On the other hand, the supporters were far from happy with their next two home games against Partick Thistle and Port Glasgow attracting crowds of 4,000, and the whole business remains puzzling even after an interval of over 100 years.

It was of course the Scottish Cup which caused all the trouble that year. It was an 'Old Firm' (as they were now called) Cup Final and as Rangers had beaten Celtic in the Scottish League on 13 March, there was a certain feeling that Rangers, with Alec Bennett now on board, were beginning to fight back, but a few early disappointing results in the League in the autumn meant that a League challenge was unlikely – and Celtic's main challengers were in fact Dundee.

A couple of days after the defeat to Rangers at Celtic Park, McMenemy gained his second Scotland cap scoring twice in a 5–0 defeat of Ireland at Ibrox. Ireland, in fact, had no answer to McMenemy who teamed up with his old friend Alec Bennett on the right wing to devastating effect. McMenemy might have hoped for a cap against England at the Crystal Palace on 3 April, but his place went to the worthy Bobby Walker of Hearts. It turned out to be a bad day for Scotland at the 'Palace of Doom' (as it was sometimes called), for Quinn misfired and Bennett was not at his best, and it is hard not to believe that McMenemy might have made a difference.

The Scottish Cup Final on 10 April 1909 attracted 70,000 to Hampden. Quinn scored for Celtic but then Rangers moved Alec Bennett to centre-forward where, taking advantage of Loney's absence through injury, he ran riot and scored twice. Only seven minutes remained when Celtic equalised, and it was a strange goal as Rangers goalkeeper Harry Rennie tried to evade a charge from Jimmy Quinn and stepped over the line.

Another draw! Another big gate – and some officials of both sides did not have the tact to keep quiet about the money that was now flowing in! Eyebrows were raised yet again and people recalled last autumn's Glasgow Cup with its amount of lucrative replays. But Celtic had another concern. After their 1–1 draw with Third Lanark on the Monday after the Cup Final, Maley realised that they still had eight games to play between 17 April (the day of the Cup Final replay) and 30 April when the season officially ended. Any extension would have caused all sorts of problems with players' contracts etc.

Maley accordingly suggested that another replay was not possible and put forward the idea of play to a finish or indeed extra time in the event of another draw. Rangers and the SFA's reply was the worst possible – they made NO reply, so the 60,000 crowd came to

Hampden in a state of confusion about whether there would be extra time or not. As it happened it was another draw – Jimmy Gordon scoring for Rangers and Celtic, inspired by McMenemy, fighting back and equalising in the second half through Jimmy Quinn.

Full-time duly came. Celtic's players thought there would be extra time and stayed on the field as did some of the Rangers players who genuinely did not know what was going on. Crucially, the referee Mr. Stark stayed on as well, encouraging the crowd to wait. No official announcement was forthcoming, and one or two fans wandered on the park with no more malign intention, at this stage, than to talk to heroes like Quinn and McMenemy. The referee then walked off with the ball tucked under his arm, (possibly having received a signal from an official in the stand to do so) taking the players with him.

What precisely happened next to trigger off an orgy of destruction has proved difficult to tie down, but within half an hour mayhem had broken out with goalposts and payboxes being burned. No violence was ever threatened to the players although it was only the quick thinking of Maley's brother which saved the Scottish Cup, and the target seemed to be (as usually happens in such irrational circumstances when passion replaces reason among the none-too-intelligent) policemen, ambulancemen and firemen. The whole thing came as a huge shock to Edwardian Scotland which prided itself on its love of law and order, and remains to this day as a potent and vivid example of the demonic power of a crowd, with the high-brow Press using words like 'ochlocracy' to describe mob rule.

The Scottish Cup had, of course, to be withheld that season, and the shame is that the publicity surrounding that event rather tended to overshadow Celtic's phenomenal winning of the League that year when they played eight games in twelve days to win the flag. They lost one, drew two and won five while poor Dundee at the top of the

League, had to sit and watch the Championship being taken away from them. McMenemy played in all the games except one and was outstanding throughout, scoring Celtic's crucial second goal at Hamilton in the final game to ensure the triumph and to collect his own fifth League medal in a row.

He would have cause to feel happy in spite of the Hampden trauma. He was now nearly 29, had won five League medals, three Scottish Cup medals and had reclaimed his Scotland place. His career had a long way to go yet. In fact, it had barely started. 1909–10 was arguably the year in which he would play his best ever football.

He won another Glasgow Cup medal in October 1909, scoring a couple (although some sources give him a hat-trick) in the semi-final replay against Queen's Park and two weeks after that, he won himself a Scottish League cap against the Irish League in a 2–0 victory at Firhill, a game in which no fewer than five Celtic players played. He was three times out with injuries after the turn of the year – once after a bruising Old Firm on New Year's Day 1910 in which he was brutally targeted by Jimmy Galt who did not earn his nickname 'Dirty Galt' without cause.

Similar bad treatment came his way at International level. McMenemy was now recognised as International material and having played creditably in the Scottish League v English League game at Blackburn at the end of February, he was duly picked for Scotland v Wales at Rugby Park on 5 March. There he was the victim of a shocking tackle by a disagreeable character with the cliched Welsh name of Llewelyn Davies, who really should have been sent off but who received his just deserts when Andrew Devine of Falkirk scored a late winner.

The injury meant that Napoleon missed the Scottish Cup semi-final next week against Clyde. Celtic lost 1–3, and most Celtic supporters were of the persuasion that if McMenemy had been playing, it would have been a different matter. Similar feelings were expressed about the next International match which Scotland contrived to lose to Ireland, but McMenemy was fit and was chosen for the one that mattered – the game against England at Hampden on 2 April 1910.

In what has been described as one of the greatest teams Scotland has ever had, McMenemy was outstanding, described as 'pure art' by some chroniclers. He scored the first goal, picking up a pass from Jimmy Quinn, and after Quinn scored the second goal, Napoleon simply took charge of the game, spraying passes with bewildering accuracy and never allowing the English midfield, the much vaunted Ducat and Makepeace to get a kick of the ball. Jesse Pennington in later years would say that he had never see such play as that demonstrated by Jimmy McMenemy at Hampden that day. It was virtually a Celtic forward line of Bennett, McMenemy, Quinn, Higgins and Templeton with only Sandy Higgins of Newcastle United never having played for the club – and even he was a self-confessed Celtic supporter!

But for McMenemy it was back to basics after that heady triumph, for a League Championship needed to be won. Celtic did this on Monday 25 April 1910 to register six League wins in a row. It would be a long time (over sixty years in fact) before that record was overtaken. Unlike the previous year, it was a comfortable win, and they could even afford to lose to their closest challengers Falkirk on the run-in!

Chapter 4

THE RETRENCHMENT 1911–1914

It is generally assumed by Celtic historians that the years from 1910 until 1914 were a poorer phase of Celtic history. This is only partially true. Rangers did win in the League from 1911 until 1913 to break Celtic's six-in-a-row run of success, but these seasons were hardly total failures for Celtic. They did manage to lift the Scottish Cup in 1911 and 1912, admittedly with no great aplomb, after a turgid couple of games in the Final against Hamilton Academical in 1911 and in a poorish game at a windy Ibrox against Clyde in 1912. Yet the failure to lift the League Championship was enough to signal to the gloomy pariahs in the Celtic support that the good days had come to an end. In fact the team were simply re-grouping and would soon be back with a vengeance.

For McMenemy, this period was a good time, both in his general play and in what it taught him about the game. Certainly it was the time that he began to win more Scotland caps, the reason presumably being that McMenemy now shone in the Celtic forward line, whereas previously, in the all-conquering six-in-a-row side, he was merely a part of it, a major part in it but not necessarily any more obvious that Bennett, Somers or Hamilton, all of whom earned their affectionate nicknames of 'The Artful Dodger', 'The Powder Monkey' and 'The Dancer' respectively from a grateful and appreciative support. And that was before they even began to talk about the man whose name dominated Scottish conversation – Jimmy Quinn!

That Celtic were faltering had become apparent by early September 1910 when Celtic managed to lose three League games in a row. A century later, this sort of form automatically leads to calls for 'regime change' and sackings of managers, and even in 1910 it was a serious matter where, although the manager's position was not necessarily under any kind of threat, new players were required. It was clear that defeats to Falkirk, Morton and Kilmarnock meant that there would be no League title this season. The defeat to Rangers in the Glasgow Cup Final on 8 October – a triumph celebrated to a disproportionate extent by the Ibrox players and supporters with the Rangers players reported as singing 'Come, Landlord, Fill the Flowing Bowl' when the trophy appeared in the dressing room, for it was their first piece of significant silverware for some time – was a further indication of problems at Celtic Park.

All good things do, of course, come to an end, and for Celtic, there were reasons. Young, Loney and Hay, the half-back line now seldom played together with Hay, in particular showing signs of being less happy with Celtic and with Maley than he had been in the past, Jimmy Quinn was now slowing down and was more and more injury prone, and Peter Somers, McMenemy's equivalent in the inside-left position had now gone to Hamilton Academical where he was fated to die a young man, but McMenemy remained virtually untouched by all of this. Indeed in the midst of all the bad results at the beginning of the season, he had been awarded a benefit, something that would guarantee his own financial security and that of his family for the next few years, and something that is perhaps undervalued in more financially secure times. It was a light-hearted affair against near neighbours Clyde and won 1–0 by Celtic through a Dan Munro goal. Sadly only 2,000 turned up, but an indication of the great regard in which Napoleon was held came when an anonymous benefactor donated a set of eleven gold medals for the winners of this game.

Jimmy remained at inside-right, supplying ammunition, winning balls and scoring a few goals himself (12 in season 1910–11), his value to the team in no way undiminished by his quiet determination to do his best for the club and by his sagacious appreciation of the changed situation. He was aware that the current set of players whom Celtic possessed were nothing like as talented as those of a few seasons previously, but he also realised that the way to bring them on was NOT to express impatience and remind them of how good Somers and Bennett had been, but to encourage them gradually and gently with mild cajoling. Shouting was not his style, which perhaps explains why he was never captain. The uncouth, loud (but still caring) Jimmy Young was perhaps more suitable for that, following the departure of James Hay.

It was during season 1910–11 that there emerged a fine right winger, someone whom Napoleon saw as a worthy replacement for Alec Bennett. This was a small, dumpy looking character who nevertheless had massive strength in both his shoulders and particularly his legs which would in later years be likened to tree trunks or to the legs of a billiard table. He was called Andy McAtee and came from Croy where he was personal friend of Jimmy Quinn. In spite of this apparent advantage, Andy remained painfully shy and sensitive and many a time after he had been on the wrong end of a shouting from Maley, Sunny Jim or even some of the crowd (who were not taking at all kindly to the passing of the League Championship from Parkhead to Ibrox), he was taken aside by Napoleon and comforted with good advice. 'Handy Andy' with the cannonball shot became one of the stars of the great Celtic side in the Great War and swore by Napoleon. It was a more current political and military figure, however, who was distressed by Andy, according to a supporters' poem:

'The Kaiser, they say, came to Glasgow one day
And said to Ludendorff 'Woe is me!'
'My German artillery's just fit for the pillory
They can't shoot like young McAtee!'

The 1910–11 season may well have been a less than total success for Celtic, but for McMenemy himself, it was a great time with even Rangers fans compelled to admit that he was the best player around in Scottish football (jokes ran around Glasgow that he would get to the South Pole long before Scott, Amundsen, Shackleton or anyone else). At last his ability began to be recognised by the Scotland authorities, for he was chosen for the Scottish League against the English League at Ibrox (a creditable 1–1 draw) on 4 March, then travelled overnight by train to Cardiff to play against Wales on the Welsh Holiday Monday (another draw, this time 2–2 and Scotland indebted to Dundee's Bob Hamilton's last minute equaliser which had its genesis in the play of McMenemy) before a fortnight later at his own Celtic Park scoring for Scotland in the easy 2–0 victory over Ireland.

On 1 April 1911, he was given his first cap against England in England. It was played at Goodison, the home of Everton. This was a fine game which Scotland claimed they should have won because they thought they had the ball over the line, before they eventually got their last gasp equaliser. The game was remarkable for several things. One was that some Scottish supporters sailed from Glasgow to Liverpool, another was that it marked the emergence of a man called William Struth, then the trainer of Clyde as a man of good managerial capability (he would of course became manager of Rangers after the war) but the interesting thing as far as McMenemy was concerned was that it was to him that the fans made the impromptu presentation of the lucky horseshoe, covered in lucky white heather of course, at St Enoch Station on departure. His team mate Jimmy Hay may well have been the captain, but to the fans, it was Napoleon who was the main man.

If Jimmy was affected by such displays of adulation, he would have been proportionately distressed by next week's crowds feelings of a totally different kind. This was the Scottish Cup Final between Celtic and Hamilton Academical at Ibrox where 46,000 people saw a dreadful goalless draw in a game ruined by high winds and a bone dry pitch, conditions which were not suitable for the youngsters on both sides. This did not excuse entirely the poor performance of people like McMenemy who must have been hurt by the cries of 'cheat' and 'fix' and a strange chant heard at full-time which went along the lines of 'another big gate'. (Memories of the 1909 riot were of course fresh in people's memories and the 1910 Scottish Cup Final had tactlessly gone to a third game as well before Dundee finished off Clyde).

Celtic made a crucial change for the replay the following Saturday involving the introduction of Andy McAtee (McMenemy and Quinn had both made an approach to Maley in this regard), but although it was a better game, there was still rather too much of a wind on a pitch made wet by a 'deluge which might have needed Noah and his Arc to counteract' an hour before the start Fortunately the rain stopped, but the wind didn't and Celtic faced the wind coming from what is now the Broomloan Road end of Ibrox in the first half. They survived that, and McMenemy now knew that Celtic only had to play sensibly and the Cup would be theirs for the seventh time.

His task lay in the calming his other forwards down, using the short-passing game and eventually with ten minutes left, he got his reward. Some intricate passing saw the ball slipped through to McMenemy who realised that all he had to do was dummy the ball and the wind would carry it through to Quinn who would make no mistake. With telepathy that was almost intuitive he jumped over the ball, and Jimmy crashed home. Hamilton Academical were unlikely to come back from that and their fate was sealed when centre-half Tommy McAteer hammered home just on the full time whistle.

McAteer, like McAtee and Quinn, came from Croy and this Final was known as the Final of the three Crojans, and the celebrations in that mining village were a sight to behold for days afterwards! For McMenemy it was his fourth Scottish Cup medal – and he was nothing like finished yet! He did however pick up an injury near the end of the season and missed the Glasgow Charity Cup games – a shame for he might have made a difference in the closely fought Final – but he had recovered enough to travel to Central Europe for the tour in May and June where the presence of a man with the name 'Napoleon' was a considerable tourist attraction for the citizens of Vienna and Prague, these rich, elegant, opulent bastions of the Austro-Hungarian Empire who could not possibly have grasped, in 1911, how little time they had left.

Ernst Kaltenbach who became a great Swiss International played against Celtic on 27 May and scored Basle's only goal of the game in a 5–1 victory for Celtic for whom McMenemy scored a hat-trick. He always felt honoured to have played against Napoleon, and more than 50 years later when Basle were drawn against Celtic in the European Cup Winners Cup in October 1963 and having heard that McMenemy was still alive, he travelled with the Basle team (sadly outclassed by the young Celtic team in the Parkhead rain before a crowd already on a high because Real Madrid had beaten Rangers earlier that day in the European Cup!) and did indeed have the privilege of meeting the great Napoleon once again!

Celtic continued to toil in 1911–12. James Hay had now gone to Newcastle, and Sunny Jim became the captain. Sunny found the new responsibility more than a little onerous and struggled to find form. Quinn was out for a while, and in the Glasgow Cup First Round replay on 13 September at Firhill, the new home of Partick Thistle, Celtic were forced to play McMenemy in the centre in a strange forward line of McAtee, Travers, McMenemy, Donaldson and Brown. It was virtually a one-man forward line and *The Glasgow Observer* has this to say 'McMenemy was zig-zagging opportunities for colleagues who could not respond. No wonder he held up his hands in despair'.

McMenemy himself was injured in a coarse game against Aberdeen on 21 October, and for two months he was on the sidelines. Celtic's form was not necessarily bad, but it was inconsistent and it was becoming clear to Maley that Paddy Travers who would in later years go on to manage Aberdeen and Clyde, was no more than an ordinary player and that in comparison with McMenemy, he was less than useful to the side. So on 2 December 1911 for a home game against St Mirren Maley introduced a slender, spindle-shanked Irishman by the name of Patrick Gallacher. This was of course the incomparable Patsy, and although men like Quinn and Loney expressed concern about the frailty of the youngster (Quinn apparently saying that Maley should have been done for manslaughter, and Loney saying that the last time he saw a pair of legs like that, there was a message attached to one of them – a reference to the method of sending messages by pigeon post), the young Gallacher did very well, including the highly flattering reference in *The Evening Times* that 'his control and passing was comparable with McMenemy's'.

Napoleon returned in time for a friendly in Belfast on Christmas Day, and the following week, on New Year's Day 1912, hopes that the Championship challenge could yet be resurrected began to be entertained after a devastating 3–0 win over Rangers at Parkhead with Jimmy Quinn scoring all three goals in a splendid forward line of McAtee, McMenemy, Quinn, Travers and Brown. McMenemy was absolutely splendid, but no more so than the rest of the team who quite simply decided to turn things on before a massive crowd of 74,000.

Sadly it was a flash in the pan, and the sad ability to draw games that they should have won raised its ugly head once again. But progress was made in the Scottish Cup against teams like Dunfermline Athletic and East Stirlingshire and more difficult opposition in Aberdeen against whom Celtic were distinctly lucky to earn a replay at Pittodrie before a more business like, McMenemy led, operation at Celtic Park saw them home 2–0.

McMenemy's International career continued with a game for the Scottish League at Ayresome Park, Middlesbrough in mid February. It was a poor Scottish performance leading to a 0–2 defeat and McMenemy was probably lucky to be chosen for the first full International against Wales at Tynecastle on 2 March. Scotland won

1–0, a late goal scored by the battered and bruised Jimmy Quinn, but the general performance of the team was such that a few changes had to be made and for the other two Internationals of the year, Bobby Walker of Hearts regained the inside-right spot.

Possibly for the first time in his career, (he was now 31) McMenemy may have felt himself under pressure, and there was an additional problem at Celtic Park. The problem was that the young Gallacher was simply too good to keep out of the team, and as he was eleven years younger than Napoleon, it made things look difficult for Jimmy.

But McMenemy was also aware that he himself was still too good to leave out, and while everyone was occupied with the Scotland v. England International on 23 April (which attracted an astonishing 127,307 crowd in spite of a rail strike in many parts of Scotland!), a quiet revolution took place at Pittodrie where Celtic were playing an insignificant League match against Aberdeen.

McMenemy (tradition has it that it was he himself who suggested it to Maley) moved to inside-left and Gallacher came in at inside-right. This allowed Celtic to have both their ball players on the same field, and the actual positions of 'inside-right' and 'inside-left' possibly did not mean very much, for McMenemy was always a great believer in interchanging. Without McNair and Quinn (both playing for Scotland), Celtic did well to get a 1–1 draw, and Maley now had a more difficult decision to make for the next game.

This was the semi-final of the Scottish Cup against Hearts at Ibrox. (1912 was the first year that neutral venues were used for semi-finals). Hearts were giving signs of returning to their glory days of last century, and in particular they had two fine wing-halves in Bob Mercer and Peter Nellies. The wing-halves would of course be expected to mark Celtic's inside-forwards, and as Celtic's inside-forwards McMenemy and Gallacher would have given away several stone in weight to the burly Edinburgh men, Maley might well have decided to drop young Gallacher (whose day would come) and go for the experienced Travers or Donaldson. But McMenemy wanted to play at inside-left to allow a chance for the precocious talents of Gallacher to let themselves be seen, and McMenemy's opinions counted for a great deal with Maley.

The labour problems which bedevilled 1912 continued and there were no special trains from Edinburgh. In spite of this, a crowd of 43,000 appeared with a huge representation of 'capitalists' (as people from Edinburgh were termed rather than those industrialists whom Karl Marx did not like!) present for a game in which most people fancied Hearts. It was not to be for the Tynecastle men, as it was one of these days in 1912 (New Year's Day against Rangers being another one) when everything that Celtic tried simply worked for them. Young Gallacher acquitted himself well, not allowing himself to be put off by the coarse tackles of Nellies and Mercer. John Brown, (the Fifer who had taken over from the increasingly frail and inconsistent Davie Hamilton on the left wing) played well, Jimmy Quinn was an excellent decoy target for Celtic, who could always rely on Jimmy to take two men with him, and the combination of McMenemy and McAtee was, quite simply, marvellous, even though McMenemy was theoretically inside-left rather than inside-right.

McMenemy scored twice before half-time with fine feeds from McAtee, and the wonder was that more goals weren't scored. Hearts were a well beaten side with their crest-fallen supporters trooping out of Ibrox before John Brown scored Celtic's third, once again an excellent example of team work. It was a fine performance by everyone and set Celtic up for their 12th Scottish Cup Final, this time against their East End neighbours Clyde who had beaten Third Lanark in the other semi three weeks previously.

Everyone had a soft spot for the Bully Wee who a couple of years previously in 1910 had been within seconds of winning the Scottish Cup. They had of course beaten Celtic in the semi and for a long time looked sure to win the Final as well. But Langlands of Dundee had equalised in the last minute, then after a replay, Dundee had won the second replay through 'Sailor' Hunter, the man who would move on to become Manager of Motherwell after the War. Clyde's own managerial team was not without significance for the Manager was Alec Maley, the younger brother of Celtic's Willie, and the trainer was William Struth, who had, as we have seen, done a good job with Scotland the previous year and was destined for other things in the future at Ibrox.

Maley decided to stick by the team which had done so well for him in that very impressive semi-final. 48,000 were at Ibrox on a day that, like last year's Scottish Cup Final, and so many others before that, was bedevilled by a strong west wind. The newspapers that morning were full of the imminent maiden voyage from Southampton of the world's largest ever sailing ship, *The Titanic*, and tended to say little about the battle between Glasgow's East End teams for the Scottish Cup.

The wind that day was less consistently from the West but tended to be more gusty and capricious at times dropping for a considerable amount of time before resuming. To say that it ruined the game would be an exaggeration, but it very definitely had an effect on proceedings. Celtic went ahead through McMenemy in the first half when an Alec McNair free-kick took a bobble or two in the wing and found itself at the feet of the unmarked Napoleon. This was in the first half, and then on the hour mark, a run and a cross from McAtee found the head of John Brown who nodded on for young Gallacher to squeeze home.

Clyde then rallied and Celtic's goalkeeper John Mulrooney was forced to make some fine saves but Celtic's half-back line of Young, Loney and Johnstone (Johnstone, another Fifer, proving a more than adequate replacement for Jimmy Hay) held out, and McMenemy was more able to tame the ball in the wind than most. It was Celtic's 8th Scottish Cup and McMenemy had won five of them.

What pleased him more than most things about this triumph was the way that his two young protegees, McAtee and Gallacher, had developed. Both owed a great deal to McMenemy and in future years neither would be slow to acknowledge the contribution that Napoleon had made to their development. Napoleon was now more than happy to play at inside-left, and there was a little more icing on the cake at the end of the season when the Glasgow Charity Cup was also won, admittedly on the rather artificial method of counting corner kicks, but as there were seven corners to Celtic as against nil to Clyde, it was clear that Celtic were the better team.

Another European trip followed, this time to Norway and Denmark where the only bad result was a defeat to the Danish Olympic XI. Celtic were much praised for their play and gentlemanly behaviour with the man called Napoleon much looked for and sought after. Once again, as he did 100 years previously, Napoleon was conquering Europe.

So what went wrong in 1912–13? Quite simply, McMenemy had a poor season with injury and loss of form, Gallacher suffered from 'second season syndrome' whereby defenders worked him out – and sometimes not too gently – and the promise of spring 1912 was not fulfilled. It would be eventually, of course, but such things take time and Celtic would celebrate their Silver Jubilee with nothing to show for it other than the Glasgow Charity Cup, won without McMenemy who by then was in hospital having knee surgery.

McMenemy's distaste for rough play was seen in an argument that he was reported to have had with George Utley of Barnsley. This was a propos of the 'friendly' game played on Tuesday 3 September 1912 at Parkhead between the Cup holders of both countries. The game was anything but 'friendly' with Barnsley from Yorkshire (where they still boast about breeding them tough with permanent chips on shoulders) attacking Celtic rather than tackling them in the relentless rain. McMenemy, who normally never said a great deal on the field or afterwards complained to Utley about the constant fouling. Utley said 'In English football, this team of yours wouldn't last a month', McMenemy replied by saying that 'In Scottish football, yours wouldn't last a match'.

He would have even more cause to be unhappy about tough tackles a couple of weeks later on 21 September at Dens Park, Dundee where he was targeted by a couple of vicious defenders and was injured shortly after he had equalised for Celtic. It was actually his arm that was hurt, caused by him putting out his arm to save himself after a tackle. It was enough to put him out of the game until early November (although he did make an ill-advised attempt to play against Clyde in the Glasgow Cup a week later) and by that time the Glasgow Cup had been lost and the League challenge had been seriously impaired.

There was the occasional good game that year – the New Year game, for example, saw Jimmy Quinn score the only goal of the day at Ibrox – but too many off days, and it was becoming clear that McMenemy was struggling with form and fitness. March 1913 saw McMenemy at his nadir, and now that he was 32, people were beginning to ask whether he was finished or not. On 1 March he was picked to play for the Scottish League against the English League at Hampden. It was a fine Scottish performance, 65,000 seeing a 4–1 win, but McMenemy did not look at his best and was not picked for any of the full Internationals.

Then a week later when Hearts came to Celtic Park in the Scottish Cup, the age-old argument in favour of who was best – Bobby Walker or Jimmy McMenemy – seemed to take a decisive shift in favour of Walker when he scored the only goal of the game, and McMenemy looked lethargic and uninterested to the disappointment of the packed crowd on whom the gates had to be closed shortly after kick-off. This was a massive blow for Celtic, and they never really recovered.

Injury kept him out of the next game against Motherwell (which Celtic lost), and then on 22 March he played what turned out to be his last game of the season, a 1–2 defeat to Falkirk at home, effectively bringing to an end Celtic's title challenge, and raising major questions about whether Napoleon was finished.

The truth was that he had been struggling for some time against injury, in this case a knee injury for which surgery would be required. This was carried out in May 1913, and although it was a success, quite a few supporters (and, one suspects, McMenemy himself) might well have wondered about whether or not they had seen the last of Jimmy Napoleon McMenemy.

But it was almost as if 1912–13 had to happen to allow for the triumphs of 1913–14, for this was a truly great season, the team winning the Double of the two Scottish competitions for the first time since 1908 – and a feat that would never again be repeated for 40 years. It was a splendid Celtic team who played competent football while McMenemy was out injured and truly magnificent football when McMenemy came back.

He took a couple of games to recover from his knee operation but then he had only completed eight games before he travelled to Pittodrie and sustained a horrendous break of the collar bone after a clash with Aberdeen centre-half Wyllie. He would now be out until almost the turn of the year, but people were beginning to ask in his absence 'Do Celtic need McMenemy?' The power of the side was truly phenomenal, but McMenemy during his recovery (he was frequently seen with the team, his arm in a sling on occasion, sitting on a train discussing tactics or applauding – with one hand! – from the balcony of the pavilion) would hardly have felt jealous because most of the success came from the men that he had done so much to bring on – Andy McAtee and Patsy Gallacher.

The left-winger was now a man called Johnny Browning (the previous one had been John Brown!) – a rough diamond, but with no lack of skill on the football field and with whom McMenemy had already struck up a rapport in spite of being totally different characters. The centre-forward spot presented a few problems for Quinn was now 35 and also out with injury, but like his friend McMenemy, assiduously helping out with the team even when he himself was out injured, and after a few less happy choices, Maley came up with a youngster called Jimmy McColl. Like Gallacher and indeed McMenemy himself, he looked frail and underweight but he would soon earn himself the nickname 'the Sniper'.

The defence began with Shaw, McNair and Dodds – and the fact that those three are still frequently quoted a century later really says it all, for they were a fine troika. Supporters who should know better then go on to say 'Young, Loney and Hay'. This is in fact not true but is an understandable combination of two great teams. Jimmy Hay had of course gone to Newcastle United in 1911 and the left-half in 1913–14 was the strapping Fife collier called Peter Johnstone, a tough character with great ball-winning skills and who would surely have become Celtic's greatest ever left-half had he not been killed at the Battle of Aras in 1917.

If Celtic fans spent an unhappy Christmas in 1913 (Christmas was no great thing in Scotland in 1913 as everyone was still gearing up for the following week's Hogmanay celebrations), they needn't have, for although they had only drawn with Motherwell on 20 December, this had brought to an end a run of 13 straight League wins in which Shaw, McNair and Dodds had conceded only two goals, and which had propelled them to the top of the Scottish League where they were fending off a strong challenge for Hearts and Rangers. Further good news came to lighten up Christmas in the rumour that McMenemy was back and that he would be playing at Ayr United in the last fixture of 1913.

Napoleon did indeed play in that game – a 6–0 demolition of Ayr United, a side who were in their first season of the First Division and clearly struggling to cope with the problems that this Celtic side could create – but it was the New Year Day fixture against Rangers at Parkhead which clearly announced that Napoleon was back. The crowd was a massive 75,000, and Celtic were a goal up as the game drifted towards half-time. Rangers claimed that their goalkeeper Johnny Hempsey was impeded by Celtic's centre-forward that day, a red-headed Englishman with the unlikely and Dickensian sounding name of Ebenezer Owers, as Sunny Jim scored the first goal, and a certain amount of resentment and tension was coming into the game.

McMenemy defused all that, for by half-time the talk was of little other than his great goal. McMenemy, being a man of all the talents, decided to try some dribbling this time beating each one of the five Rangers defenders before crashing the ball from the edge of the penalty area high into the Rangers net. The crowd, as often happens in the aftermath of such brilliance, took some time for the enormity of what had happened to settle in before 'sustained applause' broke out with even the 'Rangers partisans' agreeing that it was a good goal. Alec Bennett, McMenemy's old friend who had crossed the city divide in 1908 and now wished he hadn't, was seen to smile ruefully.

Half-time was spent with Parkhead still glowing about that goal, and in the second half, Napoleon was cheered every time he touched the ball, which was frequently, as he set up Johnny Browning for two second half goals. This was now the third year in a row that Celtic had defeated Rangers on New Year's Day and it was an excellent start for what was to be an excellent year for Celtic. No one however could quite predict everything that 1914 was destined to bring to the world.

Indeed, in early 1914, the Irish community in Glasgow were very happy. Not only were their team doing exceptionally well with heroes McMenemy and Gallacher winning game after game for them, but there was also a realistic chanced that the issue of Irish Home Rule might at last be resolved. The House of Lords which had stopped Home Rule more than once in the 19th century had now been emasculated by the resolution and constancy of Lloyd George, and the Bill was approaching Royal Assent. The Ulstermen were trying to stop it, but without success, even though they threatened civil war.

April 1914 was a great month for McMenemy. On 4 April he starred for Scotland against England in a glorious International at Hampden. He had already played for the Scottish League against the English League at Turf Moor, Burnley (a 3–2 win) and two very disappointing draws against Wales and Ireland, but this was the game that mattered. A six figure crowd and hundreds more on top of houses about half a mile away as well as those with the ingenuity to pile a mound of earth outside the ground on the North side saw a great game.

It was 1–1 at half time, and the second half was five minutes advanced when he won Scotland a corner kick on the right. (He was of course playing at inside-right that day whereas for Celtic he was still outside-left). As the corner came across and as the England defence focussed on Rangers' Willie Reid, Napoleon quietly lost his own marker and met the ball on the volley to put Scotland one-up. Twenty minutes later, he made space for himself in the centre of the field and rather than blast with his phenomenal right foot, he decided to lob the advancing goalkeeper. He seemed to have done it, but the ball hit the bar to the chagrin of McMenemy but Willie Reid was rushing in and finished the job.

Scotland thus won 3–1 and McMenemy was now the hero of Scotland. The following week however, a casual observer might have been forgiven for thinking that the Irish had taken over Ibrox, for the Scottish Cup Final was played between Celtic and Hibs. Both sets of supporters were on a high about Irish Home Rule, and such was the enthusiasm that the Hibs team charabanc was delayed by the massive crowd. Before the game began, the crowd sang 'God Save Ireland' 'with lung-bursting enthusiasm' and it was an atmosphere which unnerved even the experienced McMenemy.

It was a shame that the game failed to live up to all this hype. Gallacher and McMenemy were good in patches but the luckless Ebenezer Owers failed to capitalise on opportunities, and if anything, Celtic were lucky to get off with a 0–0 draw when Willie Smith of Hibs was through on Charlie Shaw in the last minute but was forced wide by the ever ready Charlie.

So it was back to Ibrox on Thursday. (Both teams had League fixtures which had to be fulfilled, and Hibs even played the night before!) Celtic, perhaps on the advice of McMenemy, replaced Owers by Jimmy McColl, a man who had faded from the picture since he returned from a game earlier this year and discovered his mother lying dead, and the change worked marvellously. With Napoleon in

The Celtic team of 1913-14. Jimmy McMenemy is seated fifth from left.

total control, McColl scored twice and Browning twice as well, the result was a foregone conclusion and over and done with long before some of the belated Hibs fans arrived at Ibrox from Edinburgh! Before full-time and with Celtic at 4–1 well on top, Maley was seen to stand up in his place to indicate to referee Tom Dougray to finish the game for he had no desire to humiliate Hibs.

This was McMenemy's sixth Scottish Cup medal and two days later at Parkhead, again against Hibs, he won his seventh Scottish League medal when Celtic clinched the League Championship which had been heading in their direction for some time. Rangers had won the League for the past three seasons, but there was a feeling that the League would stay in Celtic's possession for some considerable time now.

It seemed that life simply could not get any better for Celtic and McMenemy. Indeed it could and did, for Celtic then proceeded to lift the Glasgow Charity Cup as well, before going on yet another European tour which included Germany and Austro-Hungary, where there was a nasty game between Celtic and Burnley (the English Cup winners) in which McMenemy felt compelled to complain to Dick Lindley about a few bad tackles. Jimmy simply did not like the rough stuff, and it will be remembered that a couple of years earlier when Barnsley were the opponents he had a similar complaint.

Yet the 'rough stuff' was very much part of the game at that time, and one wonders what Napoleon felt like when Sunny Jim or Willie Loney was dishing out the raw meat, or indeed when Jimmy Quinn was doing his shoulder charging of goalkeepers, something at which he excelled. A quote from Willie Maley years later is worth considering in this context. 'The football pitch to McMenemy was a chess board. He was continually scheming and plotting and seldom if ever troubled himself with the physical side of the game – he had no need'.

But was Maley imagining things when he claimed several years later and with the considerable benefit of hindsight that on the summer tour of 1914 there were more men in uniform in Central Europe? And that, although the Scottish guests were always treated with respect and politeness, the welcome was not as warm or spontaneous as it had been in past years? Not that it mattered in the short-term of course, for Celtic were back in Scotland by the beginning of June, several weeks before an event in Sarajevo changed the world.

Chapter 5

WAR AND ALL ITS HORRORS

N o one could have predicted it. All the stuff about the 'two armed camps' and 'Europe being a tinder box for generations just waiting to explode' was written several years later with the benefit of hindsight when everyone had seen what had happened. A casual look at newspapers in 1914 contains no inkling of trouble brewing, other than in Ireland where the Ulstermen were turning awkward about the long promised Irish Home Rule. The Suffragettes were doing silly things like putting bombs in letterboxes, throwing themselves in front of the King's horse at the Derby and defacing paintings in Art Galleries – things that hardly helped their cause, but they were generally treated with light-hearted scorn and a certain amount of ridicule, rather than outright hostility. And summer 1914 was a glorious one with lovely weather, with Celtic supporters in particular glorying in last season and relishing the arrival of August and a return to the football.

It was a series of mad incidents that caused it all – a provocative trip to Sarajevo, a botched assassination attempt which was given a second chance, vindictive Austrian desire for a lot more than a pound of flesh, the Czar seeing some bogus pan-Slavic glory if he helped the underdog, the German Kaiser, temperamental and unstable, unable to resist a fight, the Russians calling on the French to help in accordance with some arcane treaty or entente, the French wanting to revenge the horrors of 1870 and to win back Alsace and Lorraine, and finally the Kaiser's deranged desire to invade Belgium, even if he knew that it meant a fight with the British Empire of which his cousin was king, and war with the country of his granny, the late Queen Victoria.

And how everyone suffered for this craziness! Yet to an extent, the peoples of Europe had themselves to blame for it all because they embarked on the idea with such enthusiasm! It was fun, adventure and a chance to escape the slums and the poverty back home. One wonders what McMenemy made of all this. One suspects that he did what he always did on the football field. 'Keep the heid, Celtic' would have been the cry.

Maley and Celtic read the situation well. Maley, the son of a soldier in the British Army, did of course support the war effort, encouraging recruiting campaigns at Parkhead and other things, but he was particularly careful to see that his fine team of 1914 were all working in jobs, such as mines and shipyards, which would have made it easier for them to resist the emotional blackmail of the self-righteous. Maley was no fool. Some of his men, notably the heroic Peter Johnstone would indeed join up and be killed, but the main reason that Celtic would win the Scottish League in 1915, 1916, 1917 and

1919 (and losing it only narrowly in 1918) was that Maley managed to keep his fine side together.

Other sides reacted differently. Hearts for example enlisted virtually en masse in late 1914, a brave if perhaps misguided gesture which has been much praised and eulogised by later writers, and many other clubs actively encouraged their men to join up on the grounds that the club would benefit from the reflected glory, and even if it meant that the team itself did not do as well as it might for the next couple of years, well, did that really matter in the context of the need to teach Johnny Foreigner a thing or two? In any case the war would be 'over by Christmas', or so they said.

The role of football in wartime is often misunderstood by football historians. It is often thought that no one really bothered with it, that it was a sideshow, that it somehow didn't matter. To a large extent this is true in the context of what was going on in the rest of the world, but one must not think that sport, football in particular, was considered trivial by supporters at the time. Attendances were, in the circumstances, remarkably high and news of games were awaited with eager anticipation by the men in the trenches and on the High Seas, for there was little else to make anyone happy or cheerful. It is indeed probably true, as they said, that among Scottish soldiers at least, Patsy Gallacher was indeed 'the most talked about man in the trenches'.

That said, professional football was severely emasculated. The Defence of the Realm Act, the hated 'Dora' insisted that before any man could play football for money he had to have a war-related job, and as a five and a half day week was usually strictly enforced with men working until mid-day on a Saturday, there were obvious problems of men getting to football grounds in time for kick off. Eventually the distant teams of Aberdeen, Raith Rovers and Dundee would be compelled to drop out of the Scottish League for the last two seasons of the war.

Internationals and League Internationals ground to a halt, although the Scottish League was a wheen more reluctant to give up than the SFA and kept going with League Internationals in season 1914–15, and for some strange reason the Scottish Cup was suspended – something that deprived McMenemy of a few more medals, but the Scottish League continued as did the two Glasgow competitions (because, presumably, they did not involve much travelling) and there were numerous representative games like Glasgow v An Army XI in aid of Belgian Refugees.

Guest players were allowed – Stanley Seymour, for example, destined to become a giant in the history of Newcastle United, cut his teeth for Greenock Morton because he happened to be stationed there – and quite a few famous English Internationalists would appear for other teams, often under the pseudonym of Smith or Brown, something that Rangers did with notorious success in 1918. Recruiting drives were held at various games in the early years until conscription became the norm in 1917, and for soldiers home on leave, attendance at their local team's fixture was a visit to be much prized and looked forward to. Indeed wearing the uniform would often entitle a young man to free admission at some grounds and he would be looked upon with much respect and indeed admiration, not least by female supporters.

In spite of all this, there was a strong 'Football must stop' lobby with righteously indignant letters to *The Glasgow Herald* asking why these 22 young men were not in uniform, and did this sort of thing not simply encourage to shirkers and the cowards to run away from the action? Maley frequently went on the defensive about all this, stressing how his team played games to help the war effort, sent footballs for the boys in the trenches and how a game of football to a soldier on leave was an indication that the world was still normal; indeed that it was part of a way of life worth fighting for.

Men like McMenemy may have suffered the occasional jibe about 'cowardice', but he was as aware as anyone about how he was doing a good job in the shipyards. He could of course have given in to the emotional blackmail of Kitchener's pointing finger that 'Your country needs you', but he would have noted with a rueful sigh the numbers of men who did what Kitchener said and then found themselves involved in the British Army's blackest day – the Somme on 1 July 1916. Indeed, as we shall see, he would have personal reason to be aware of the follies of militarism.

Lloyd George himself, admittedly with hindsight, would acknowledge some 20 years later when he wrote his memoirs that blanket recruitment was a huge mistake, and that all those shipwrights, fitters, engineers, blacksmiths, plasterers and bakers who fell at the Somme, could have been doing a far better job on the home front. The Somme, of course, proved nothing other than the ruthless savagery of 20th century warfare and the gross incompetence of some of the British generals. The famous quote about the British Army being 'lions led by donkeys' was by no means wrong.

Curiously, the Irish situation, something that was becoming a major issue in 1914 with the Home Rule Bill, and which certainly was a fundamental part of the folklore of the support after the war, did not seem to effect Celtic or their supporters during the war. The Easter Rising of 1916 was of course presented one-dimensionally by the British Press who persisted in saying that the rebellion lacked support among the working class in Dublin. In any case it was swiftly and brutally repressed, and even the executions, although they did raise an eyebrow or two among the more fair-minded of the British population for their sudden and summary nature, were quickly relegated to obscurity as other horrendous events elsewhere in the War took over in the Press.

Consequently, given the necessity to win the Great War, there was perhaps a slight downturn in 'Irishness' at Celtic Park during the war years. It would however return with a vengeance very early in the 1920s when the vicious deeds of the Black and Tans became known, and when Terence McSweeney and Kevin Barry took their place in the pantheon of Irish heroes. For the moment, however, the War kept going on relentlessly, the casualty lists mounted inexorably and very soon everyone knew of some family who had sustained some loss. The main focus and desire was on the end of the War, even though it might mean defeat and even though it might mean, as some like John McLean, the icon of 'Red Clydeside' devoutly hoped, a total change in regime.

The whole thing, of course, caught everyone by surprise. Saturday 1 August was the first time that anyone really spoke about a war which might effect 'us', but even so, cricket matches were played and people still went on their holidays, although the Glasgow Fair had now finished. By 3 August France was at war, and on 4 August, as the Kaiser failed to stop his crass invasion of Belgium, Great Britain had to follow suit.

Thus the Celtic Sports in 1914 on 8 August went ahead with the country actually at war, and the predominant emotion being one of excitement that something thrilling was in the air. A few of the older men who had been at the Crimea some sixty years earlier tried to exercise caution, but everyone else from all social classes, all age groups, both sexes and all ethnic groups were mad on the idea. In some cases, they couldn't get to the recruiting offices quickly enough!

The football season itself opened on 15 August, and war or no war, Celtic fans travelled to Edinburgh to see the opening fixture at Tynecastle, and formed a large part of the 20,000 crowd on the day that Hearts' new stand (which still of course exists as the Main Stand) was formally opened. It was a tasty fixture with more than a little animosity between the two sets of fans, but it was Hearts day. It might have been different if Hearts goalkeeper Archie Boyd had not saved Jimmy McColl's early penalty, but Hearts opened the scoring, and then late in the game when Celtic were pressing for what would have been a not undeserved equaliser, Hearts scored again.

It was not one of McMenemy's better games, as he himself admitted. Perhaps he took the hostility and proximity of the Hearts crowd rather badly. They seemed to think that now that the country was at war, a nickname like 'Napoleon' was particularly inappropriate! *The Glasgow Observer* makes the acid comment that 'For downright one-sidedness and sheer hostility, there is nothing to beat a Tynecastle crowd'. It is a comment that could be made with equal validity in the twenty-first century.

There was of course no 'phoney war' in 1914, as there would be in 1939–40. The Battle of Mons took place before the end of August and soon after that, troops were heavily involved in the action to save Paris and northern France (large parts of Belgium had already fallen into the hands of the Hun) at this very early stage of the war, and it would be some time before the trenches could be built and the conflict would become its terrible war of attrition.

Celtic's form that autumn was inconsistent. Injuries compelled changes and at one point McMenemy was deployed at centre-half. McMenemy was of course a player who could play in most positions – indeed he was one of those who advocated that a player should indeed be ubiquitous, but a 0–2 defeat by Clyde at Shawfield in the Glasgow Cup in September (a result that 'caused consternation in the forces' when news reached there) perhaps indicated that centre-half was not exactly McMenemy's position. He was simply too small, too easily knocked about, and now that he was over 34, did not quite have the mobility. In addition, there was no scope for him to display his creative side.

After the middle of October with most injuries healing up and McMenemy and Gallacher back on song, the form of the team picked up, and eleven games were won on the trot including a McMemeny-inspired defeat of Rangers by 2–1 on Halloween in which Jimmy scored the first goal and controlled things throughout.

But McMenemy (and Celtic) sustained a severe blow at the end of November when it was announced that his old colleague and fellow inside man, Peter Somers had died at the age of 36, not from any war-related issue but after the amputation of his leg for something that sounds like diabetes. Peter was the first of that great forward line to pass away, and his funeral was well attended by all of Scottish football, for he was a much liked and somewhat underestimated and undervalued player.

Christmas came and the war that was going to be 'over by Christmas' was manifestly not so, but what there was was a very exciting race for the Scottish League Championship with Hearts, building on their good early start and earning a great deal of goodwill by the decision of so many of their players to 'join up', setting the pace, and Celtic in hot pursuit.

But Celtic had a very bad day at Ibrox on New Year's Day 1915. The 1–2 defeat by Rangers was bad enough, but it was all the more galling because Celtic controlled the game and should have won it but for defensive errors. This left Celtic four points behind Hearts (whose game was not played that day) but it was in times like this that the wisdom of McMenemy came into its own. His normal 'Keep the

Heid, Celtic' was heard on the field, but so too were his words of quiet and sage advice to the younger members of the forward line particularly Patsy Gallacher, brilliant but infuriatingly inconsistent at times, and Johnny Browning, by nature a wild boy whose prodigious talent needed to be reined in and harnessed. Napoleon was the very man for this task.

At the end of January 1915, Celtic seemed to have blown their chances of winning their second successive Scottish League. They were four points behind Hearts when the Edinburgh men came to Celtic Park on 30 January, but the game finished a 1–1 draw, something that with only eleven games left, seemed to give Hearts a decided advantage. It was a remarkable game for several reasons. One was that it attracted a phenomenal crowd of 55,000 (who should all have been 'in the trenches' according to the more hysterical of readers' letters to *The Glasgow Herald*). Nevertheless, about 10,000 of the 55,000 were in khaki, either on leave, or about to go overseas, or they were perhaps Englishmen based in the Glasgow area with a Saturday afternoon off.

They were given the treat of seeing a remarkable game of football described quaintly in *The Glasgow Observer* as 'something between and International and a Cup-tie' – two types of fixture not seen in this season. Hearts had scored first through inside-left Harry Graham and held it until half-time. Celtic turned it on in the second half however and when Andy McAtee equalised within ten minutes of the restart, it was felt that they could go on to win the game. But Hearts held out, and both teams were given a rousing reception as they left the field, with Hearts obviously the happier team. No one knew it at the time, but when Jimmy Quinn walked off the field, it was his last game of his career. Indeed he would not have been playing in this game had it not been for an injury to 'the Sniper' Jimmy McColl.

In circumstances like this, for the rest of the season with the destiny of the League flag not entirely in their grasp, all the team can do is win their own games and hope that the other teams can defeat the opposition. This would famously happen 53 years later in 1968 when Rangers stumbled under the pressure of Celtic always winning, and it happened here in 1915 as well with Hearts beginning a long and melancholy tradition of throwing away League Championships. They would do this in 1959, 1965, 1986 and 1998, for example. Whether the same would have happened in 1915 if they had always been able to call upon their best players is open to question, but from a Celtic point of view, no praise is high enough for the Celtic team who now won their next ten games and drew the eleventh, when it no longer mattered.

Perhaps it is from 1915 that dates the irrational and hysterical hatred of Celtic and all their works by Hearts fans. Certainly for years afterwards, sneers about 'war dodgers' and 'Maley's malingerers' (in addition to the traditional ones of 'Fenians' and 'weegies') were a common form of insult, for so many of Hearts' players had joined up while Maley's squad was remarkably intact.

Sniper McColl returned to form and fitness in February and soon started to find the net, scoring in eight out of the eleven remaining games, including a fine hat trick in a snow storm against Raith Rovers in late March. McMenemy himself found the net with regularity and with McAtee, Browning and Gallacher all performing well, it was a fine Celtic run-in to the end of the League.

For Hearts the stumbles began on 20 February when, as Celtic beat Dumbarton 1–0 with a goal from the Sniper, they themselves played a great game of football against Rangers but lost by the odd goal in seven – a result that meant a great deal to the Ibrox men who had had little enough to celebrate of late. The following week as Celtic got the better of Partick Thistle at Firhill, Hearts struggled to get a point in the Edinburgh Derby at Easter Road. Further points were dropped before a big blow-up (0–2) at Cappielow against the strong Morton (replete with Army and Navy stars) on 10 April as McMenemy scored the only goal of the game against Aberdeen for Celtic, and Celtic finally clinched the League on 17 April when, with McMenemy rampant and Gallacher unstoppable, they put four past a poor Third Lanark side.

For Celtic, it was a fine weekend, although the news was somewhat muted by the death in Dumfries of their legendary founder Brother Walfrid. He would have been delighted to know that the team that he created had now won the Scottish League 12 times in the 25 years of that organization's existence. It was in some ways, however, a hollow triumph in the unreal circumstances of War, but there was little that anyone could do about that. Indeed the War, so far from being 'over by Xmas' or even 'Easter', would very soon take a decided turn for the worse with a botched, ill-thought out crazy idea of Winston Churchill that attacking the Dardanelles and Gallipoli would somehow deliver a knock-out blow to the Kaiser!

McMenemy himself had now won eight League Championships in the 13 years that he had been with the club. He could claim a great deal of credit for this for himself, but he was always a modest man, content to play the game he loved for the club he loved and above all in 1915 glad that he was not in the Army. His reserved occupation in the shipyards made sure that he would be unlikely to be called up even if conscription was to be introduced. At the moment, it was still all about volunteering, and McMenemy was always able to resist the pointed finger of 'Your Country Needs You'. Not only did he have a wife and young family to think of, but he also loved playing football for Celtic.

No full Internationals were played that season, and it would also be the last season of League Internationals. There were three of them, and McMenemy played in all three – a 1–1 draw against the Southern League at Millwall in October, a 2–1 win against the Irish League in Belfast in November and a dire defeat by the English League at Celtic Park in March. This game attended by a 44,000 crowd was one of McMenemy and the Scottish League's worst ever performances, and the 1–4 defeat meant that the Scottish League did not try very hard to get League Internationals re-instated! It was pointed out, not without justification, that the trip to Belfast for example on a Wednesday afternoon was a colossal waste of manpower and transport that might have been used for purposes more suited to the war effort.

The 1914–15 season ended with Celtic maintaining their very fine record in the Glasgow Charity Cup which they had won every year since 1912. They beat Queen's Park in the First Round, then Partick Thistle (by counting corners) in the semi to set up a Final tie against Rangers at Ibrox (Rangers won the toss to choose the venue) on 8 May, a day that was not to be without its significance in the context of the War. This was the day when news reached Glasgow and indeed the rest of the world of the sinking of the RMS *Lusitania*.

This fine ship had been built on the Clyde and was sailing from neutral America with a passenger list of civilians including many women and children. It was sunk by a German U boat off the coast of The Old Head of Kinsale in Ireland with the loss of over 1,000 lives. It was not quite the slaughter of the innocents as British propaganda would make out, for the Germans had advised people not to sail on the grounds that it also contained weapons and armaments for the Allied war effort, but it was still a despicable, cowardly act which further demonised 'the Hun'. It would eventually play its part two year later in persuading the USA to join the war.

The ship had sailed from New York on 1 May heading for Liverpool and met its doom on Friday 7 May. News was vague in the morning papers but more detailed accounts began to appear in the early editions of the evening newspapers as the 40,000 crowd made their way to Ibrox for the Charity Cup Final. Thus the crowd were angry and full of justified anger. The fact that the ship had been built on the Clyde was all the more poignant for the Glasgow crowd, many of whom would have taken part in the actual construction. Thus everyone would be seething at the villainies and evils of 'the Hun', (Yes, even Rangers supporters in 1915 did not like the Huns!) and the Army cashed in on the situation by delivering a strong recruiting speech urging yet again more young men to join the fight against the 'fiendish Fritz' and the 'butchers and beasts of Berlin'.

It was difficult to concentrate perhaps in such an atmosphere on the football, but it was a surprisingly good game with, for McMenemy, a triumphant ending. Joe Dodds opened the scoring for Celtic with a long-range shot which deceived everyone, but then with Patsy Gallacher off injured, Rangers scored twice before half-time, a lead that they maintained until well into the second half even when Patsy came back, although clearly half-fit. In such circumstances, Celtic needed Napoleon more and more and he did not let them down.

Probing and passing as always, McMenemy gradually got the better of his direct opponent Jimmy Gordon and within the last ten minutes, slipped the ball through to Johnny Browning to level the score. It now looked as if the game would be settled on corners in which Celtic may just have had the advantage but with time fast running out, a long ball from Tommy McGregor seemed to be drifting across the Rangers penalty area when it eluded everyone except McMenemy. McMenemy for a small man had a surprisingly high jump, and rose to nod the ball past Hempsey in the Rangers goal.

Rangers had no time to come back, and McMenemy had won yet another medal. The season finished the following week at Hampden when Celtic beat the Rest of the League 1–0 in a game organized by the Glasgow Corporation for the Belgian Refugees Fund. 50,000 were there, all still upset about the *Lusitania* and all spouting out foul-mouthed bile about how much they hated the Germans and all their works.

The new season opened of 1915–16 with Celtic winning 10 straight games in a row, and this is all the greater an achievement when one considers some of the problems that confronted some of Celtic's players. But before the season started, everyone at Parkhead had great reason to be proud of an ex-Celt called Willie Angus. Willie, who hailed from Carluke, had not been good enough to play for the first team and joined up at the start of the War. He was gazetted for the Victoria Cross 'for most conspicuous bravery' to go with the already won Distinguished Conduct Medal. He gained this for rescuing a friend of his (also from Carluke) under heavy fire, losing an eye in the process, and continuing to engage the German trenches. This had happened at Givenchy on 12 June 1915. Willie would always be given a standing ovation whenever he returned to Parkhead, as he did many times before his death in 1959.

The Glasgow Observer gives some hint of the atmosphere of war-time football when 'Man In The Know' details the team's visit to Dens Park, Dundee on 18 September 1915. He is talking about the arrival of the Celtic team at Dundee's West Station and their walk up to Dens Park.

When we landed (sic) in Dundee, it was as if a mistake had been made and we had found ourselves somewhere in France. There were soldiers and sailors everywhere, kilts and trews, terriers and regulars, officers and privates all moving about excitedly and animatedly, most heading in the direction of the football.

The 'terriers' were not, of course, some breed of dog, but the Territorial Army. They were normally of course Reservists, but were being called more and more into action after the dreadful losses of the regular army in 1914 and the early part of 1915. It is to be hoped that they felt entertained by the McMenemy-inspired 2–0 victory for Celtic, for less happy days were imminent for the good people of Dundee who were fated to sustain dreadful casualties at the Battle of Loos.

Tragedy had hit Alec McNair, a tragedy no less poignant for not really being part of the War. Alec's wife died just at the start of the season, leaving poor Alec to cope with five children. But Alec was not called 'The Icicle' for nothing. After being out for a few weeks and showing indifferent form on his return, he soon learned that he had no monopoly on misfortune, buckled to his task and with maximum support from the strong family and community of Larbert who gave him help with the children, Eck worked his twelve hour shift in the munitions industry, brought up his kids and continued to play with some excellence for Celtic. As the Scottish poet Lewis Grassick Gibbon might have put it, 'Ye need smeddum for that!'

And the war came a lot closer to McMenemy himself, when his brother was killed at the Battle of Loos in September 1915. By coincidence Joe Dodds' brother died a few days later at this terrible battle, and Maley had the job of comforting both men. But McMenemy's 'Keep the Heid' philosophy came into play here as well, when he looked at men like McNair, Dodds and Willie Angus, then looked at the crowd which still followed Celtic in massive numbers and reckoned that most of them would perhaps also be suffering some grievous hardship. They therefore needed something to cheer them up, and good football as played by this superb Celtic team would be a great tonic to all concerned.

Death notices from the Battle of Loos were still filling the newspaper columns when Celtic met Rangers in the Final of the

Glasgow Cup on 9 October 1915 at Hampden. Soldiers and sailors were admitted free, and the crowd seemed to be well in excess of 75,000, according to one account. Another says 'about 25,000', the truth being somewhere between these two extremes, one imagines. They saw a vintage Celtic performance with the score, amazingly, only 2–1 for the green and whites as Gallacher and Browning scored in the first half, and then Jimmy McColl (having a rare bad day) missed a barrowload of chances in the second half, as McMenemy totally dominated proceedings with 'long and accurate passes' Even though there was only one goal in it, Rangers fans streamed from the ground long before the finish as Celtic registered their first Glasgow Cup victory for six years.

'Man in The Know' in his column 'In Celtic Inner Circles' in *The Glasgow Observer* is impressed by the attitude of both McMenemy and Dodds. 'For I need not tell you that these two great comrades, McMenemy and Dodds, were companions in sorrow'. They would have been excused from playing in the circumstances, but the Celtic community needed them – and they provided. A glance at the death notices in *The Evening Times* throughout these awful months of September and October 1915 will show that McMenemy and Dodds were by no means alone in their sorrow.

One normally did not beat Rangers and escape scot-free, and McMenemy sustained a bad leg injury. He really should not have played for several weeks, but another injury, this time to the precocious McAtee, compelled McMenemy to play in the next game against Hamilton, out of position and with his leg bandaged up. They won that one, but lost the next two with McMenemy out of the St Mirren game altogether and struggling, manifestly unfit, through the next game which was a 0–3 defeat to Rangers at Ibrox.

Worse followed on 13 November at Tynecastle, but the sullen faces who travelled back on the over-crowded trains from Haymarket to Glasgow that night, would have been cheered if they had known that they would not lose another game for almost eighteen months, and that two League Championships, two Glasgow Charity Cups and another Glasgow Cup would be won before Celtic bowed the knee again!

McMenemy's injury problems resolved themselves and he became Mr. Consistency once again as Celtic settled to a game once more. By New Year's Day 1916 (they drew 2–2 with Rangers at Parkhead) they were on level terms with Rangers, and although McMenemy missed the next three games with injury, by the time he returned, Celtic had seized a strong grip of the Championship, as Rangers slipped up to Partick Thistle and Hearts showed a tendency to draw games that their supporters expected them to win.

February and March 1916 were particularly good for this slick Celtic outfit with only one goal conceded and that was in a game that Celtic had beaten Hamilton Accies 5–1! McMenemy of course master-minded most of all this, so much so that he seldom attracted the headlines any more. It was as if this was what was expected of Napoleon.

It was the events of 15 April that attracted attention far beyond Scotland. Celtic won the Scottish League – it had been obvious that this was to happen for some time, but seldom has a League Championship been confirmed in such a way. An unseasonal fall of snow on 25 March had put paid to the game between Motherwell and Celtic. The problem was when to play it, for League football would not be allowed in midweek (other than the Holiday Monday, and that was already spoken for because Third Lanark were due to come to Celtic Park that day), for fear of the effect that it would have on the war effort. Similarly no extension of the season would be allowed beyond the end of April – for only charity games and friendlies were allowed after that.

Sunday was also out of the question for religious reasons, so the only solution was to play the game at Motherwell on the Saturday evening, after the games Celtic v Raith Rovers and Motherwell v Ayr in the afternoon! Contrary to belief in some quarters, this was not the first time in these straitened war-time circumstances that clubs had to play two games in a day, but this was the first time that the games had been played with such panache and distinction.

First in a game that kicked off at 3.15 pm Celtic beat the hapless Raith Rovers (even though they contained the future Rangers player Sandy Archibald in their ranks) 6–0. That game finished about 5.00 pm, one imagines. An hour later at 6.00 pm, Celtic kicked off against Motherwell at Fir Park, not even having bothered to change their boots for the short charabanc trip to Fir Park. The evergreen McMenemy scored the first goal in the second game, which struggled to finish in daylight, and even that was with having no half-time break. Celtic won 3–1, and made only one change. 'Sniper' McColl was out injured, so Joe O'Kane played in the first game and scored twice, then was replaced in the second by a young man, stationed at Scone Military Camp near Perth. He was called Joe Cassidy and already dubbed 'trooper'.

The Scottish League now won, Celtic then drew 0–0 with a much depleted Hearts side who had several of their side listed (for propaganda purposes, one imagines) as Private Wilson and Sergeant Miller, for example, and then on the Holiday Monday (when football was permitted) Celtic beat Third Lanark 4–1 with Joe O'Kane scoring a hat-trick and ex-Celt Davie McLean guesting for Thirds and scoring their only goal. Spectators returning from the game might have bought an evening paper and discovered that there was some sort of disturbance in Dublin, centred mainly on the GPO in Sackville Street. Whatever it was, it was soon dealt with by Dublin Castle and by the team that Celtic finished their League season by beating Partick Thistle 5–0 it was all over.

The Glasgow Charity Cup now took centre stage with Rangers (much changed, bringing back Alec Bennett and introducing Stan Seymour from Morton as their guest) coming to Parkhead to lose 0–3 to goals from McMenemy, Young and McAtee in a game in which Celtic were seldom troubled, and then on Saturday 13 May Celtic lifted their fifth Glasgow Charity Cup in succession with a 2–0 defeat of Partick Thistle, McMenemy having played in them all. By this time, a few eyebrows were beginning to be raised (and not only among the Irish community) about the relentless executions of the Irish rebels who did not seem to be allowed a fair trial. Yesterday, for example, the Scottish Socialist James Connolly from Edinburgh, a Hibs supporter, one presumes, but a man with a great admiration for the achievements of the Celtic had been shot, and rumours were spreading that he had had to be brought in to Kilmainham Gaol by ambulance for his execution, for he had been wounded in his defence of the GPO.

But this was soon buried in other news, and Celtic themselves, who had won every competition they entered for that season, then sustained a rare defeat. It was a friendly, but a prestigious one when 50,000 saw them lose 0–1 to the Rest of the League in a match for War Relief. Thus ended the 1916 football season, and the mad summer of 1916 took its place. There was the naval Battle of Jutland – indecisive but costly, and then the appalling slaughter of the Battle of the Somme took place from 1 July onwards, something that proved nothing other than that the British Army's leaders, all educated at private schools, had a criminal ignorance of military strategy, matched only by their callous indifference to the lives of their soldiers. A hundred years previously, they claimed that the Battle of Waterloo was won on the playing fields of Eton. If this is true, a generation of young men in 1916 all perished in the same place!

The football season started again in August as news from France continued to be dire. Football had now established itself once again in that it was no longer under attack from the morally correct and the religious extremists, but it was now much reduced with teams fielding young lads, veterans, players who were clearly not fit, and such were the vagaries of war-time transport that players could not guarantee to arrive on time. Often queues at pay-boxes would hear a cheer as one of their favourites charged his way through the crowd to get stripped in time for kick-off.

Celtic's half-back line of Young, Johnstone and McMaster which had served them well since 1914 now broke up. Peter Johnstone and Johnny McMaster had gone to the war and were only available when on leave, and Sunny Jim Young injured his knee against Hearts on 30 September 1916, effectively ending a Celtic career which had lasted more or less as long as McMenemy's. But Napoleon was still there, leading the line with his usual aplomb and making the newcomers in the half-back line Jimmy Wilson, Willie McStay and Hugh Brown feel as if they had played for Celtic all their life. If any of them were in awe of McMenemy, there was no need for them to be, for he remained his humble, supportive and knowledgeable self.

Both McMaster and Johnstone were available for the Glasgow Cup in the autumn. 50,000 were at the semi-final when Rangers came to Parkhead. Peter Johnstone had travelled all the way up from England overnight, such was his determination to play, and several others on both sides looked tired and jaded, something that was hardly surprising for they had been working in the morning. It was thus a dull game, but Napoleon, conserving his energy better than the younger men and benefiting from the necessarily slower pace of the game gradually brought out the best in Andy McAtee, releasing him time and time again to send over inch perfect crosses. The first goal from just such a McAtee cross which beat everyone except Johnny Browning, then McMenemy fed O'Kane to charge through the middle (just like Jimmy Quinn used to do) to score the second, and then with time running out and the Celtic fans in great voice, McAtee once again picked up a McMenemy pass to cross for the head of Peter Johnstone who thus proved that his emergency journey from Aldershot was indeed necessary and productive.

Two weeks later in the Glasgow Cup Final, Celtic completed the job by beating Clyde 3–2 in a game that was less even than the scoreline should suggest, for although Clyde scored first and last, Celtic hit a blistering spell in the middle of the second half with three goal in ten minutes which knocked the stuffing out of Clyde. McMenemy once again played a part in the lead up to each goal.

Celtic continued more or less invincible in the Scottish League. There were a few draws but they survived the calendar year of 1916 undefeated, and well into 1917, something that was more praiseworthy when one considers that they had to come through most of the winter without Patsy Gallacher. This was because of bizarre circumstances, and although one is often cautious about allegations of unfair treatment and does not always wish to feed the Celtic paranoia, nevertheless, it is difficult in this case, not to see a hint of draconian justice.

Patsy Gallacher had been fined £3 for 'bad timekeeping' at his job at John Brown's Shipyard in November. This was a fair punishment of course under the infamous Defence of the Realm Act, although for a newly married man, £3 was a lot of money. Nevertheless, Patsy paid up and the matter seemed to be at an end, until the Scottish League saw fit to fine Celtic £25 for apparent complicity (ie they played Gallacher while knowing that the case was being judged) and suspended Gallacher from playing football from mid-December 1916 until the end of January 1917.

Words like 'outrageous' do not quite seem to cover this, for Patsy's offence had nothing to do with his playing football. Had he been playing for Celtic when he should have been working in the shipyard it would have been a different matter, but there was no logic to this at all. There was a little sympathy for Celtic in some areas of the Press, but with the war now approaching its third Christmas, there were other things for people to be concerned with. It did look however (and continues to do so almost a century later), for all the world, like a piece of revenge and spite.

In Gallacher's absence, it would not be true to say that Celtic struggled. Their unbeaten record remained intact as Shaw, McNair and Dodds showed the world how good a defence they were, but there was perhaps a lack of fizz – 1917's New Year's Day game at Ibrox was a boring 0–0 draw and a similar result happened the following day against Clyde. McMenemy too appeared to share in the general lethargy, clearly missing the creative play of Gallacher with whom he had developed an almost telepathic understanding, but also perhaps affected by the war-weariness that seemed to affect almost everyone after the horrors of 1916 when the British Army had sustained its most fearful calamity at the Somme, the British Navy was failing to stop the U-Boat menace and there did indeed seem to be 'A long, long trail awinding into the land of my dreams' as one of the popular songs of 1917, immortalised by the great Irish tenor John McCormack, would have it.

Gallacher's return in February 1917 immediately galvanised Celtic into action. Celtic fans saw six wins and two draws, enough to carry them to the Championship on the early date of 7 April when they won 3–1 at Dumbarton at the ground that was once called 'fatal Boghead'. The Russian Revolution was now of course in full swing and Rangers collapsed 'just like the Czar did last month' as a newspaper of the time pointedly put it to Third Lanark at Ibrox. It was Celtic's fourth League flag in a row, and the only slightly unhappy note came when they surrendered at last their unbeaten 66 game unbeaten record when Kilmarnock beat them 2–0 at Parkhead on 21 April (after the League had been secured).

Discerning spectators would have noticed a new flag that day at Parkhead – not any of the League Championship flags, nor the old flag of Ireland with the Harp, but the flag of the United States of America. This reflected the changed nature of the War, for the United States had now joined the Allied side more or less at the same time as Celtic won the League. The Czar of Russia had indeed been forced to abdicate and would spend the next year vainly begging his relatives in Britain for political asylum, and continued Russian participation in the war was a matter of some doubt under its Provisional Government. This had however been compensated by the arrival of the largest and wealthiest power on earth, the USA, now irked by the continuous German torpedoing of ships in the Atlantic and weaned away from its traditional isolationism to join what President Woodrow Wilson himself called 'the European slaughter-house'.

The Allies would now eventually win, but it would be a long time, next year in fact, before the Americans would be there in any sort of strength to make a difference. Their potential arrival did give the sagging war effort a boost. Celtic now finished their season in the traditional way by winning the Glasgow Charity Cup beating Rangers and then Queen's Park in the Final, so that 1916–17 must join 1915–16, 1907–08 and 1966–67 as being seasons in which Celtic won every competition they entered. Boring perhaps to lovers of other teams, but to Celtic fans, at home and abroad, a tremendous boost to morale.

But Celtic were to suffer a grievous blow in France. As fans made their way home from the charity game on 26 May in which Celtic lost to the Rest of the League, rumours began to spread that stretcher bearers at Arras had failed to bring back any trace of Peter Johnstone who had played for the club in the Glasgow Cup Final in October and had then gone overseas to serve with the Seaforth Highlanders. In one of the repeated 'pushes that would take us to Berlin', Johnstone had seen action at a place called Arras in mid-May and had not been seen since. He was confirmed dead on 6 June, but has no known grave other than his name on the Arras memorial.

McMenemy was clearly upset by all this, but once again reckoned that everyone suffered in war. He himself had been lucky in being allowed to play football for the club he loved all those years, and although he was now 37 at the start of the next season, he still felt that he had a great deal to give. But with conscription now in force, it would be more and more difficult to avoid the draft. He was already on 'deferment', and he might yet have to join up. Yet he felt that his job in the shipyard would have been important enough to keep him out of the forces, especially when one considered his age.

Season 1917–18 was the first season in which McMenemy struggled with fitness and form. It was also perhaps hardly accidental that it was also the season in which Rangers at last regained the upper hand over Celtic, although many supporters felt that it was because of the wealth of English talent that Rangers Manager William Wilton was able to bring into the club to play in key matches. Celtic on the other hand began to look jaded, something that was hardly surprising in the wake of such sustained and deserved success.

McMenemy sustained a serious leg knock in a game against Partick Thistle on 17 September 1917 and was compelled to hobble off after less than half an hour. Celtic won the game with two goals from Jimmy McColl, but a Press comment on the second half (with Napoleon watching from the Celtic Park balcony) was revealing 'Celtic abandoned the close-passing game for dashing, daring, never-say-die football after half-time'. This seems to be a euphemism for hard tacking, hard running aggressive football, the antithesis of the elegant stuff that Napoleon specialised in.

In his absence (McMenemy would be out until 10 November) Celtic lost two League games to Kilmarnock and Airdrie and a disastrous 0–3 defeat to Rangers in the Glasgow Cup semi-final highlighted how much Celtic missed McMenemy. He was only back for three games (all of them won) when he was out of the game again, falling awkwardly on his wrist in a game at Easter Road against Hibs.

He missed a game on 15 December at Motherwell when Celtic were compelled to start the game with only ten men, for Alec McNair's train was late. McNair never did arrive and Arthur McInally (elder brother of the famous Tommy) was eventually given a game. Remarkably Celtic won 4–3, but it highlighted the increasing problems of finding eleven fit men. McMaster was now in khaki and Dodds and McAtee soon would be; a new centre-half called Willie Cringan was arrested after a game for desertion and being unable to find identity papers, and to cap it all, Jimmy McColl was in hospital with appendicitis.

Other teams suffered these sort of trauma as well, and Celtic turned the New Year in 1918 ahead of Rangers, but January was peppered with draws and it was noticeable how seldom the newspapers singled out McMenemy. Yet he scored the occasional 'net-buster', and proved his versatility again by being prepared to play at centre-half if necessary for the game at Partick Thistle on 9 March. Fortunately the huge crowd delayed the kick-off and Jimmy Wilson was able to get there on time.

Celtic remained ahead and looked as if they might yet win their fifth consecutive League Championship until an old bhoy came back to haunt them. This was McMenemy's old friend Davie McLean. McLean was now registered with Sheffield Wednesday but because he was engaged on war-related work on the Clyde, he was allowed to play for Third Lanark (next year he would play for Rangers). On 23 March, just a couple of days after the Ludendorff offensive was launched on the Western Front (Russia had now surrendered and Germany was able to commit all her men to the breaking of the British and French trenches), Celtic lost 1–3 to Third Lanark. Gallacher scored a great goal for Celtic, but McLean, famous for his cannonball shooting, scored a hat-trick and Celtic had now lost their lead to Rangers, who were equal on points, but had a better goal average.

It was one of McMenemy's poorer games, as he himself would admit in later years, but once again he rallied the team to beat Kilmarnock and Hibs. Annoyingly, Rangers won as well and thus the final Saturday of the League season, 13 April, saw both Rangers and Celtic at home against Clyde and Motherwell respectively. With Rangers on top on goal average (goals for divided by goals against), McMenemy was aware that a Celtic win would not necessarily be enough, and that a win by a huge margin was necessary.

Sadly Celtic lacked a goalscorer – Quinn was long retired, McColl was still recovering from appendicitis, Cassidy, who had played when on leave a couple of weeks ago, had now gone back to France and

Adam McLean was in the centre. Adam would in the 1920s become a brilliant left-winger, but he was no centre-forward, and in any case Celtic were up against a Motherwell team who had no great desire to leave holes in their defence even if it meant giving up any intentions of scoring goals themselves for long periods of the game.

Celtic Park had a large crowd of 25,000 that day, all of them very aware that the War was now going very badly for the British Empire. The 'march back' was now on, as Britain fell back in front of the last desperate but at the moment pitilessly and relentlessly successful German offensive, the Russians could not help as they were now out of the war, the French, not for the first time seemed to be on the point of collapse and the Americans had not yet landed in sufficient strength to make any difference. Indeed there were bitter jokes hurled at the Americans who would 'fight to the last British soldier' and who really should be in France to discover what the phrase 'wild West' actually meant.

General Douglas Haig, the villain of the Somme and amazingly still in command, issued, from his safe French chateau, his famous edict on Thursday 11 April (two days before Celtic's run of four League titles in a row came to an end) to the exhausted British soldiers who were now beginning to wonder whether surrender might not be an option and who earnestly asked the question 'What was the difference between victory and defeat?' Haig both cleverly and callously using the sort of imagery that Churchill would use in the next war stated, 'There is no course open to us but to fight it out. Every position must be held to the last man: there must be no retirement. With our backs to the wall and believing in the justice of our cause each one of us must fight on to the end. The safety of our homes and the Freedom of mankind alike depend upon the conduct of each one of us at this critical moment'.

Stirring stuff, but one wonders whether it made a huge amount of difference to the war-weary soldiers or civilians on the home front. The feeling was growing that this war might yet drag on well into the 1920s, and that perhaps the Russians who had now deposed their worthless leaders and monarchs were showing the world the way forward. This affected not a few of the Celtic crowd that day, but more were simply depressed and worn down by life, not in the slightest bit cheered up by the arrival of spring.

In addition to this pessimism, the flags at Parkhead were at half mast for the great Dan Doyle, the wild rover of the 1890s who had died recently. There was a fierce determination in the air, especially after Patsy Gallacher scored first, but then tragically on the point of half-time, Rankin equalised for Motherwell. No one knew how Rangers were doing (although rumours, both true and false, spread like wildfire) and all Celtic could do was try to win the game and score as many goals as possible. Napoleon tried his best, but sometimes felt slow and less than totally fit, and Celtic, for all their shooting from almost impossible angles, failed to beat Rundell in the Motherwell goal. The game ended 1–1 and very soon the evening newspapers would confirm the more pessimistic of rumours, namely that Rangers had indeed beaten Clyde 2–1 and would therefore take the League Championship.

Those who lived through the agonies of the last days on the League season of 2003 and 2005 will appreciate how Celtic felt. It was an agonising way to finish a League season and McMenemy would not have been assuaged too much by winning the one-off War Fund Shield trophy at the end of the season, nor the seventh successive Glasgow Charity Cup Final on 25 May when Gallacher and Browning scored the goals which beat Partick Thistle 2–0. McMenemy had played in six out of these seven Finals (he missed 1913 through injury), and had made his mark on each one of these six.

June 1918 was significant for two things. One was that Britain had seemed to have withstood the German offensive, and was even fighting back, and McMenemy seemed to have decided to retire. Those who thought that Britain would now win the War were correct, but those who thought that Napoleon would no longer be seen on a football field were very far wrong indeed.

Chapter 6

THE INDIAN SUMMER 1918–1922

W hy Napoleon 'retired' in summer 1918 remains a mystery. He was suffering from knee trouble, but there was no reason to give up the game altogether, it seemed. He still had a few years left in him (as events would prove) and although he would have been 38 at the start of the 1918–19 season, men of that age were hardly unusual in Scottish football in the unreal circumstances of the war with so many of the younger men still abroad.

As it was, McMenemy, although no longer playing for Celtic, was not entirely inactive on the football front, including some sources say, a few friendly games for Linfield in Northern Ireland when perhaps his war work in the shipyards took him to Belfast. Linfield are of course traditionally the 'Orange' team of Belfast and some people feel that McMenemy would not have been welcomed there, but that is to look at things through the perspective of later on in the 20th century. In 1918 a great name like McMenemy would have been welcomed, wherever he went, and it is doubtful whether in any case, the sad identification of Linfield with sectarian politics would have started by that time.

McMenemy lived in daily expectation of the call up. *The Glasgow Observer* of 3 August says that Celtic will need a new right wing because 'McAtee is already at the front and McMenemy is under starter's orders'. A week later we are told that McMenemy was working at Ayr in the munitions industry because his knee problems made both football and soldiering impossible, hence his non-appearance at the Celtic Sports, something that was still, war or no war, going strong.

Men who had worked in reserved occupations were now increasingly being called upon and even men well into their 30s were being enlisted. Although the situation was slowly turning in the Allies favour in Europe, men were still required both in that theatre and elsewhere, particularly Mesopotamia where the enemy were the Turks rather than the Germans and although casualties were fewer than in Europe, they were still significant. The main problem was of course climate and disease, rather than shell and cannon fire.

In Europe, progress was slow, but the Americans, now at last in the field in significant numbers, were making a difference. Their leadership was as naïve as the British and the French had been, but they did have equipment, wealth and manpower. At home throughout Great Britain, deprivation and war-weariness continued, as the casualties did not stop with now almost everyone in Scotland knowing of someone who would not come back. But there was still jingoism and patriotism with the stress on how evil the Hun was.

Health was now becoming a problem on the Home Front. It was probably a rhetorical exaggeration to say that Britain was ever on the verge of starvation, but, such had been the menace of the U-Boat in the Atlantic, there were restrictions and shortages of various kinds of foods. And it was of course at this time that another of the Four Horsemen of the Apocalypse – Plague – reared its ugly and lethal head.

This came in the form of what became known as the Spanish Flu – so called because Spain, which had stayed out of the War, had proportionately more casualties from the disease and it was therefore more publicised in Spain. It first appeared in March 1918 and lasted for well over a year. It of course flourished in the horrible conditions of trenches, troop trains and ships and quickly spread to the large cities where in addition to the pre-existing slums and primitive health facilities, there was the problem of a population seriously debilitated and enervated by the lack of the proper vitamins.

The actual figures for Glasgow are hard to find, but it appears that McMenemy was one of the victims. In fact he may have been carrying the disease for some time. He was certainly less energetic than normal in the last few games of the 1917–18 season and had looked lethargic and uninterested. He was hardly the only one in this respect, of course, but this constant feeling of being below par may have been one of his reasons for this decision to retire from professional football.

In early September however a list of men appeared in *The Evening Times* who had appeared before the Sheriff to be told that under DORA (Defence of the Realm Act) any further exemptions or deferments were not possible and that they would have to join up within three months. The 'three months' time seems to be a little generous – in other parts of the country it was 'one week' – and may perhaps indicate that the Sheriff felt that the presence of McMenemy in khaki may not have been totally vital to the winning of the war, which now, in autumn 1918, seemed a matter of weeks away. As it was, all that this probably meant was that McMenemy continued his munitions job on the Clyde or in Ayr or Belfast, but he now was technically under military orders.

We now hear little more of McMenemy until after the war was over, so we must assume that he never made it to donning the khaki. He didn't play for Celtic either. But the week after the war finished on 11 November, *The Glasgow Observer* in its edition of Saturday 16 November says that:

> *It is possible that McMenemy will have his job in the shipyard taken over by a returned soldier and find himself free on a Saturday afternoon. The presence of the Parkhead Foch (sic) would make victory more certain...*

The reference to Foch made a change from Napoleon. This was the French Marshall Ferdinand Foch who was commander in chief of the Allied Armies, and who had, only five days previously 'negotiated' the Armistice which effectively won the Great War! In fact he had dictated terms. It was a highly flattering comparison.

Indeed, such was the atmosphere of euphoria that some Celtic fans went along to Firhill on 23 November (the game against Clydebank on 16 November had been postponed because of fog) believing that they might see the return of McMenemy, for optimistic rumours were sweeping Glasgow that he was coming back. He didn't play as it turned out, and *The Glasgow Observer*'s 'Man In The Know' gives them the chilling and terrifying reason why McMenemy was not playing that day.

Those who had expected to see McMenemy play at Firhill are not likely to have that pleasure for quite a long time. Mac (sic) was seriously – I might say dangerously – ill on Saturday and in fact it was touch and go, for the kind of influenza hovering around at the present is what one would call virulent. I believe the favourite has got the turn for the better, though it will still be long ere he gets back to delight us with those clever touches that mean so much and look so simple.

The Spanish flu was now, of course, rampant throughout Scotland. Willie Cringan was also reported to have flu but McMenemy's dose seemed to have been bad enough for *The Glasgow Observer* to concern itself about it, even in the midst of all the 'celebrations' of the end of the war. But what celebrations?

Glasgow was a strange place that November. Characterised by 'pea-soup' fog as it was called, more or less all month and still very much on a war footing with troops arriving and departing from the various railway stations, there was very little rejoicing for the Armistice. Even Lloyd George himself would call 1918 in his memorable phrase 'the blood-stained stagger for victory', and there was rather too much evidence of that in the sight of seriously wounded and disabled soldiers being disembarked from Central Station on their way to Yorkhill or some other hospital to convalesce. A few would recover totally; many would live on for a few years with permanent reminders of the horrors of war; some would die a few days later after the trauma of the trip home, having at least the consolation of seeing their wives and mothers before they died. If this was a victory, one would not have liked to have seen a defeat.

In the midst of all this, there was political discontent, seething away – and not without cause. Labour troubles had been hidden by the Press, but they would not go away. A rent strike was in progress, and the imminent release of the Socialist leader John McLean from Peterhead (he would arrive back to Buchanan Street Station in early December to a hero's reception with thousands of supporters present) made the authorities uneasy, and it seemed to be no accident that so many soldiers, most of them longing to be home and out of the hated khaki, were hanging around Glasgow, just in case there were to be political disturbances. The Prime Minister, Lloyd George had called a General Election for 14 December. He was secure in the knowledge of an easy victory for his Coalition, for the opposition had had no chance to organise with so many of their men still in the forces, but it was widely suspected that there would be a great deal of trouble in the New Year.

In these circumstances, rumours spread, alarmist and ridiculous ones – that Germany had regrouped, that there was to be another war this time against Russia, that curfews and house arrests were about to become common practice in Glasgow. Even in football, strange things began to be heard, namely that Jimmy McMenemy, had not only recovered totally from his flu, but was in fact coming back to play for Celtic, now that the war was over and that he would not now be called up. That one was no rumour. It was the truth. He was tolerably fit by 7 December, but probably did well to miss the trip to Motherwell where the team went down 1–3, but he was ready for the Dumbarton game at Parkhead on 14 December.

In fact, 14 December was the day of the General Election (the first one ever that women were allowed to vote in) and it was also the day of the return of Napoleon. Willie McStay (or McStey as some newspapers spelled his name) was also now back from war service, and 10,000 were at Parkhead that raw midwinter day to see the Grant Stand and the Pavilion rise to give prolonged applause for the return of the heroes. And how fitting it was that McMenemy, having lost none of his sharpness, laid on the first goal for 'Sniper' McColl, and then scored the second himself in the comfortable 2–0 win over Dumbarton.

Celtic fans were ecstatic. From the doggerel verse of 'The Reconstructed Celts':

With a reconstructed side
Celtic met Dumbarton's pride
And their mastery to one and all was plain
How the Celtic faithful cheered
When Napoleon re-appeared
And McStey turned out for the Celtic once again

to the chortlings of 'Man In The Know' – 'the very fact of McMenemy turning out had the effect of spurring on the others' 'long ago it was not so much what McMenemy and Somers did – and they were always doing somebody (sic) – as the amount of work they got out of their comrades', it is clear that his return revivified the beleagured Celtic community. Comparisons were made between Napoleon and the young Dumbarton players (some of them very young because there had been a struggle to find a team) 'It is the other chap who is done. The old one plays out time as fresh as a yearling, though hard at it since 1903'. Even more sober analyses of McMenemy's play agree that he 'showed the unhasting sureness and easy control which, allied with his unfathomable swerve, made him the despair of opponents'. And then as an afterthought – 'Dumbarton played him fairly'!

This was from a man who only three weeks before was 'touch and go' with the flu! He now however bent himself to his duty. Celtic were still behind in the League race to Rangers, having played some poor games this season, notably on 7 December in that 3–1 defeat at Motherwell, but, although Patsy Gallacher was still out, the fact that Napoleon was back galvanised the team and the support. On 21 December, the team came from behind to beat Hamilton at Douglas Park, and then with Gallacher and McMenemy restored to the inside positions, the team played 'the best they had played all season' to beat Hibs 2–0 at Celtic Park on the last Saturday of the momentous year of 1918.

65,000 were at Ibrox on New Year's Day to see the first Old Firm clash since the ceasing of hostilities, but one would not have thought that the war had ended, such was the predominance of khaki in the crowd. Indeed quite a few English soldiers had their first taste of Glasgow football, and there were even one or two curious Americans who had heard so much about this game that Scotsmen talked about so incessantly. Celtic, boosted by the sudden return on Hogmanay of Joe Cassidy on leave from the Black Watch, dominated the first half and it was McMenemy who side-glanced a header from a Cassidy cross to put Celtic ahead, but Rangers equalised late in the game to retain their current advantage of five points, even though Celtic had a game in hand.

There then followed a supreme Celtic effort of winning fourteen and drawing two of the next sixteen League games. Andy McAtee was back from his reluctant stint in the forces in the Italian Alps in mid January, and with Patsy Gallacher returning from various injuries at about the same time, the team was virtually back to what it had been in 1914 with Adam McLean now replacing Johnny Browning on the left wing. This was hardly to the team's disadvantage. Attendances seemed to increase more or less by the week, as more and more soldiers came back from the war and expressed their delight at the sight of Napoleon in the team – the 38 and a half year old Jimmy

McMenemy whom many thought had given up the game and of whom quite a few people had heard stories that he had died of the Spanish Flu in November. But reports of Nap's death were greatly exaggerated. Indeed he was more alive and more in control of that wonderful Celtic team than ever before.

Once or twice in early 1919, trouble, of the political sort, seemed not too far away. 1 February saw Celtic beat Kilmarnock 2–1 at Parkhead in an atmosphere that was tense with strains of *The Red Flag* clearly heard coming from the crowd. Some changed the words to *The Green Flag*:

Where'er we go, we'll fear no foe
Our songs will fill the earth and sky
At Ibrox Park and Cappielow
We'll keep the Green Flag flying high!

But for those who sang the original words, there was little doubt that this song was aimed at the police who had played a despicable part in the suppressing of the George Square demonstration of the previous day in what became known (with a little exaggeration) as Bloody Friday. The Scottish Secretary of State openly expressed his fears of Bolshevism, and although troops were not visible at Celtic Park that day – there might have been serious trouble if they had been – everyone knew that they were on alert and could be summoned at short notice.

Ireland too, now that the war was over, became an issue once again. Sinn Fein had captured 75 of 105 seats at the General Election in December, and now refused to take part in the Westminster Government, setting up instead its own Parliament or Dail in Dublin. Celtic supporters were therefore edgy and excited, and really not a little confused about what was going on, but there was little need for confusion about what was going on on the field, for apart from draws against Motherwell and Morton, Celtic won all their other games, usually with a great deal of ease. A 4–0 defeat of Falkirk, for example, caused the writer of *The Glasgow Observer* to remark that 'Celtic's game was like their pre-war work and beautiful to witness'.

As is often the case, football being the psychological game that it is, this caused Rangers to tremble and drop points, and eventually the 15th League Championship (and McMenemy's 11th) was won after two difficult away fixtures at Hearts and Ayr, the Ayr game played in stifling heat as Celtic beat the Honest Men 2–0 on the late date of 10 May 1919 to win the Scottish League Championship by one point from Rangers.

For McMenemy, this represented an astonishing revival of his career and indeed his health. Indeed, such had been his form that he was chosen to play for Scotland twice in the Victory Internationals against England and once for the Scottish League. This was for no other reason than that he was still the best inside-left around. In the Scottish League game, for example, at Ibrox, he teamed up with Alan Morton of Queen's Park to mesmerise the 65,000 crowd which included a huge amount of limbless soldiers who were 'well positioned to watch the game' in what became a conscious effort by most clubs to look after the war wounded, a huge bunch of men most of them still in their 20s and now more or less totally dependent on their families to look after them.

There was also a display of either folly or nobility (depending on one's perspective) on 19 April – the day of that fine Celtic performance against Falkirk already referred to. Patsy Gallacher was chosen to play for Ireland in a Victory International, and McMenemy for Scotland. Celtic refused Gallacher permission to play, as they were entitled to do in that strange season when the country was neither at war nor entirely at peace. McMenemy then decide to balance things a little by withdrawing from the Scotland squad for 'business reasons'. This may have had something to do with one of his public houses, (he was now the licencee of a bar in Duke Street) but the far more likely reason was that both Gallacher and McMenemy wanted to play for Celtic!

There was still no Scottish Cup that year, but the equivalent was the Victory Cup a trophy in which Celtic, on a day that McMenemy was out injured, lost to the eventual winners St Mirren in a lacklustre performance at Love Street in late March. Also in that year, all good things must come to an end and Celtic's remarkable run of seven successive Glasgow Charity Cup wins fizzled out with a surprise defeat from Queen's Park in which this young man that everyone was talking about, Alan Morton, played a great part.

Season 1919–20 was the first official post-war season with the return of the Scottish Cup and full Internationals. It was also McMenemy's last season for the club, and by the end of the season he could no longer be guaranteed a place in the team. New players had emerged, notably at centre-forward a precociously talented fellow from Barrhead by the name of Tommy McInally, and Joe Cassidy 'the Trooper' who had played for the team during the War from time to time could no longer be denied a place at inside-left. Gallacher was out for a spell at the turn of the year, and needed cover, but after he came back, it was difficult for McMenemy, now approaching his 40th birthday to force his way back into the side.

Curiously the Scottish selectors did not always agree with the Celtic ones. McMenemy played against the Irish League in November, and then twice in March he played at Celtic Park in the blue shirt of Scotland – once in a full International against Ireland when Scotland won 3–0 and the following week for the Scottish League against the English League when a 0–4 belting effectively put paid to any hopes he might have had of a game for the full side against England the following month.

The Ireland game was significant, for he was 39 years and 154 days on 13 March 1920, something that made him the oldest outfield player ever to play for Scotland, and although a few goalkeepers were older, he retained this record for over 90 years until David Weir of Rangers beat it in 2010. No one would have commented on his age that day, for he was as 'spry as a younker' as a newspaper put it, distributing passes all over the field, a few evoking gasps of admiration from the 39,757 crowd as they landed accurately at the feet of a colleague from a distance of 40 yards. Andy Wilson, Andy Cunningham and Alec Morton scored the goals as the sadly outclassed Irish, even with Patsy Gallacher playing for them, were overwhelmed 3–0 in Scotland's first official home International since April 1914 when McMenemy played a glorious part in the subduing of the English. The Czar, the Kaiser and other potentates had come and gone since that day (not to mention millions of ordinary people), but Napoleon was still there!

1919–20 was, in truth a disappointing season for Celtic, but McMenemy won his last medal for the club when wins over Rangers, Queen's Park and Partick Thistle saw Celtic lift the Glasgow Cup. But there were bad days too, notably the 3–0 defeat to the emerging Rangers team at Ibrox in October and the 1–0 defeat to the same opponents in the Scottish Cup in March 1920. Inconsistency dogged the team, and although there was a late challenge for the League, it was not enough. On 6 December 1919, however, Celtic beat Motherwell 5–0 at Parkhead, McMenemy scoring twice. The second goal was McMenemy's last for the club, and it probably means that

McMenemy, at the age of 39 years and 56 days became Celtic's oldest ever goalscorer, a distinction that he still holds to this day as far as can be ascertained.

25,000 appeared on Tuesday 6 January 1920 for McMenemy's Testimonial to see a Celtic XI playing a Bradford XI, organised by Napoleon's friend Davie McLean who now played in Yorkshire. Men like Jimmy Gordon and Jimmy Bowie of Rangers, Alan Morton of Queen's Park and Andy Wilson of Dunfermline played for Celtic, and Joe Cassidy, Jean McFarlane and the famous Welsh wizard Billy Meredith turned out for Bradford. It was light-hearted stuff, ended up a 3–3 draw, Napoleon pocketed £1,000 and was cheered on and off the field in a moving and eloquent token of just how much he had meant to Celtic the past 18 years.

As this season came to an end, speculation grew about whether McMenemy would be kept on. Celtic were on one of their economy drives (misguided and unnecessary, for they were by no means poor) and it was felt that there was no role for McMenemy now that he seemed to have lost his place in the side. But the end of the season came and McMenemy was still on the pay roll. There was indeed a place for McMenemy, as it seemed. In the past he had done a great job to nurture the talents of Andy McAtee and Patsy Gallacher. There was now another talented but headstrong youngster called Tommy McInally who was giving signs that he would need a little handling if the best was to be got out of him. The young Tom had lost his father at an early age, and needed an older man to help him along. McMenemy seemed to be the ideal person for the job, and indeed had already established a relationship with the 'boy wonder'.

It was all the more surprising therefore that Celtic announced as late as 20 June 1920 that McMenemy was being given a free. McMenemy, stoic as ever, did not appear to want to throw any tantrums and would have grounds for believing that six Scottish Cup medals and eleven Scottish League medals was enough for anyone realistically to expect. What would he do, now? Glasgow did not have too long to wait for a couple of days later, Partick Thistle announced that McMenemy had now signed for them.

Was his departure premature? Possibly not, as far as playing goes, for he was now almost 40, and could not really have believed that he would be an automatic first team choice, but he was still a great mentor, a wise head with a famous catch phrase of 'Keep the heid, Celtic!' He would now be moving further north in Glasgow and it would have to be 'Keep the heid, Thistle!'

Partick Thistle had been founded in 1876, and had now settled at Firhill since 1909. They had done well to survive when so many other Glasgow teams hadn't, but they were very aware that as things stood at the moment in 1920, they had not won a single major tournament. Managed by a crusty character called George Easton, they were always hard to beat, and even as early as 1920, Thistle had the reputation of being unpredictable, and 'Firhill for thrills', which became a cliché in the 1940s and 1950s was already current. They had been elected to the Scottish First Division in 1902 and had tended to be around the middle of the table, apart from a couple of bad seasons, 1909 when they were last and 1913 when they were second last. But there was no automatic relegation in those days, and indeed it would be 1970 before that fate hit them.

McMenemy was of course given a great reception by the Maryhill crowd, and no less a reception by the Celtic crowd when he played against them. Season 1920–21 was a fair season for Thistle in the League – they finished sixth, but in the spring of 1921 it was the Scottish Cup which lit up all the Partick supporters in north Glasgow, not least because of the sheer amount of ties that were played. Three games were required to dispose of Hibs, they then had a lucky escape from a spirited East Stirlingshire side whom they beat 2–1, then another three were needed to get the better of Motherwell before yet another three games had to be played against Hearts. This made a grand total of ten games, before they reached the Final. It was to be an all-Glasgow affair, Rangers were the opponents and the game was to be played at Celtic Park on 16 April.

McMenemy had played most of the season, although now well past his 40th birthday, he was prone to injuries, and the week of the game saw Thistle wonder whether to play McMenemy or not. In the end, he got the nod, in view of injuries to other players and with the belief that an old head was perhaps required, not least because the game was to be played at his old stamping ground of Celtic Park.

Frankly, not many people gave Thistle much of a chance. Rangers were already the League Champions in all but name following Celtic's poor performance against Raith Rovers the previous week, and their great forward line of Archibald, Cunningham, Henderson, Cairns and Morton was expected to rip Thistle's defence apart. The attendance was a poor one of 28,294 and can partially be explained by the feeling that it would be an easy game for Rangers. There were other factors as well – a rail strike which made it very difficult for non-Glaswegians to attend, the reluctance of Rangers supporters to be seen at Parkhead, and the weather which was raw and cool, although by no means as bad as it could have been.

There exists footage of this game on British Pathe News. Very little of the football is seen because of the cameraman's understandable desire to capture the crowd who would then come to the cinema the following week to see themselves. But we do see the teams come out of the Parkhead pavilion, Rangers first – obliged to wear white because of Partick Thistle's navy blue with the large thistle (it would be the 1930s before the distinctive yellow and red of Thistle would become the main strip) then Thistle with McMenemy (or the man who most closely resembles him) running out third last. A couple of disabled war veterans are in the front row, and as Thistle come out, the distinctive homburg hat of the host Willie Maley (never a man to miss a photo opportunity!) is seen. We then see the captains shake hands with the referee Mr Humphreys of Greenock, a few glimpses of the play and that is about it!

It was, by all accounts, a poor game. Johnny Blair scored the only goal of the game for Thistle, and for the rest of the game, Thistle were called upon to do some desperate defending. In circumstances like this, a man like McMenemy is worth his weight in gold, for if he can get the ball, he can take it for a walk, waste time and give the defenders a breather. He avoided one or two desperate tackles from brutal Rangers players who were seeing their chances of the Scottish Cup (which they had not won since 1903) disappear, and his joy at the full time whistle was great, for he had now seven medals, more than anyone else apart from Charlie Campbell of Queen's Park who won eight, but one of them was in 1884 when the opposition Vale of Leven failed to turn up!

Once again, McMenemy was the hero of the hour, and he was allowed to keep the ball. When he got home that night, if he could have counted, he would have found 11 Scottish League medals, 7 Scottish Cup medals, 8 Glasgow Cup medals and 9 Glasgow Charity Cup medals – a grand total of 35 medals. He reputedly said to his wife, 'What will I do with this one?' Rose McMenemy smiled and replied 'Oh, just put it in the drawer with all the others!'

But then in summer of 1921, McMenemy, no stranger to European tours with Celtic, broke new ground when he went on tour of Canada and the USA. This was a big step for a man who was seldom out of Glasgow and the surrounding area, (like Jock Stein who claimed to get homesick whenever he passed Baillieston on the road to Edinburgh!) but he was invited and he went. Celtic had of course toured Europe several times before the Great War and Maley had always hankered to cross the Atlantic. Nothing however had happened, and it was actually Third Lanark who first organized this tour, under pressure from the many Canadian and American soldiers who had lived in Scotland and England temporarily during the war and who were fast developing an interest in the game, wishing more and more to see players from the country that was without much doubt the best football playing country in the world – Scotland.

But Third Lanark had problems in persuading all their players to go – in the event there were only four Cathkin men – and they had to supplement their players from players from other teams. McMenemy was invited to 'sign' for Thirds for the duration of the summer, and after a little hesitation decided to join the party of sixteen men who sailed from the Broomielaw in early May on a voyage which would in 1921 take five days – if the weather was good. Alec Bennett, now of Albion Rovers, was going and the idea of renewing his partnership with Alec must have been a great attraction.

Between 21 May and 21 July, the team loosely described as 'Scottish League' 'A Scotland XI' 'Third Lanark and Guests' or even 'Scotland' played 25 games and won 24 of them, usually by a comfortable margin against enthusiastic but outclassed opposition (some of whom had no clear knowledge of the rules of the game), who were in awe of 'Scotland'. McMenemy's reputation had of course preceded him, and wherever he went, loads of Celtic fans sought him out, asked for his autograph and tried to get their picture taken with the mighty Napoleon. McMenemy played 17 games, mostly in roasting heat, and scored five goals.

On his return to Scotland, McMenemy's remarkable career continued, and he could with justification claim to be a British Cup winner, for on Monday 19 September 1921, Thistle arranged a game against Tottenham Hotspur, the winners of the English Cup. Thistle won 3–1, and the Saturday before that, McMenemy had come very close to putting Celtic out of the Glasgow Cup, but had to settle for a 1–1 draw.

In two seasons, McMenemy played about 74 games for the club, and even that does not include a short loan spell at Stenhousemuir. Partick Thistle clearly appreciated his talent, and for season 1922–23, he was promoted to player/coach, but in summer 1923, he decided that enough was perhaps enough, and that it was time to concentrate on his other interests in the licensing trade. He would take a break, at least, from football.

Remarkably little is known for certain about Jimmy's life outside football. We know that at one point he owned a pub called 'The Duke' at 209 Great Eastern Road, but whether he still owned it in the 1920s is unknown. At other times he owned a pub in the Gallowgate and in London Road. He certainly would not have been a poor man, for he had earned a great deal from his footballing career, especially from his testimonial in 1920, and it is likely that he would have used this money to invest in the licensing trade as so many ex-players did and continue to do. It is also, of course, possible, that he resumed his job in the shipyards, for he had done this during the War.

There seems to be little doubt as to how he spent his leisure time, for football was his life. No doubt every Saturday afternoon was spent watching Celtic, but he would also be very aware of the footballing progress of his three sons, John in particular who joined Celtic in 1925. Between 1932 and 1934, Jimmy was working for Partick Thistle. In April 1933 *The Daily Record* describes 'Jamie (sic) McMenemy Partick's International Coach watching Lesmahagow v Larkhall Royal Albert League match at Craighead Park. He was impressed by Beaton and Collins, two of Jamie Ritchie's Raploch Park productions. And Jamie knows a good player when he sees one.'

Great things however still beckoned for Napoleon.

Chapter 7

NAPOLEON'S SECOND COMING

The original Napoleon came back as well. His exile on the island of Elba was not a success as far as the Allies were concerned, for he escaped and came back to France to regain his Empire and to give the British and Prussians a great deal of bother before his eventual crushing defeat at the Battle of Waterloo in 1815. This Napoleon's return was far more successful and lasted a longer time.

Indeed, not enough has been said about Napoleon's contribution to the great Celtic side of the late 1930s. He was nominally trainer, but such was the disposition of the now ageing and ailing Willie Maley that McMenemy was virtually in charge of the team, particularly during the long absences of Maley through illness and Maley's increasing obsession with writing his book 'The Story Of The Celtic' (an excellent and very valuable tome but one which took up an inordinate amount of his time), that McMenemy was 'de facto' manager.

Let it be said from the outset that this Celtic team of the late 1930s was an excellent side. Maley deserves a great deal of credit for finding these players, but it was McMenemy who moulded them. In truth, it would have to be said that they were not quite as good as the teams that McMenemy played in in the 1900s and 1910s, nor indeed Jock Stein's team of the late 1960s, but they were still an excellent outfit with only a few blemishes (Scottish Cup defeats against St Johnstone in 1936 and Kilmarnock in 1938) putting them in the 'silver' status along with Martin O'Neill's side in the early 2000s, as distinct from the 'golden' status of 1908 and 1967.

Their achievements are all the more remarkable when one considers that McGrory retired from playing in 1937 and at about the same time Willie Buchan was transferred, inexplicably other than for sheer money grubbing reasons on the part of Maley and the Directors, to Blackpool. Thanks to McMenemy, their loss was hardly noticed as McMenemy brought in men like Johnny Crum, John Divers and in particular, Malcolm MacDonald, so that the transition was seamless.

So what exactly was the relationship between McMenemy and his old boss Willie Maley? In the first place, there was a tremendous love and respect for each other – McMenemy had been if not Maley's best ever player – there was, after all, stiff competition from Gallacher, Quinn, McGrory and many others – certainly one of them. He was probably the most intelligent and the man with the best 'people skills', and McMenemy, for his part, was aware that he owed almost everything to Maley's technical and tactical know-how.

But Maley was a changed man since his heyday before and during the Great War. He was a man with personal, family problems, totally devoted to his beloved Celtic, and it was often said that he could not cope with death, particularly the premature death of so many of his great players. Peter Somers died young in 1914 , Peter Johnstone was killed in France in 1917, Sunny Jim was killed in a motor bike accident in 1922, John Thomson died on the field at Ibrox in 1931 and Peter Scarff died of tuberculosis in the Bridge of Weir Sanatorium in 1933. Each of these events affected him deeply, and a form of depression took over him from time to time. Still a deeply religious man with frequent trips to Lourdes and regular attendance at Mass, he was often struck with a form of catatonic lethargy – as the form of the team in the years between 1932 and 1934 would sometimes indicate.

In addition, he became more and more despotic with age. He had always been authoritarian, as McMenemy himself would know. McMenemy's friend David McLean would often say that the real reason that he (McLean) left Celtic in 1909 to continue his career with Preston North End was not because of McLean's religion (McLean was a nominal Presbyterian from the East of Scotland) but because of Maley's bullying attitude to players with even great Celts like Sunny Jim, Jimmy Quinn and Willie Loney on the wrong end of a severe tongue lashing after a bad result.

In the 1920s, men like Willie Cringan, Johnny Gilchrist, Joe Cassidy and Johnny McMaster might have stayed a little longer if they had been dealt with more tactfully, whereas Tommy McInally was indulged just rather too much. By the 1930s, this trend continued with Willie Cook and Charlie Napier clearly falling out with Maley and departing, with the added ingredient by now of Maley becoming nostalgic. Not without cause would he boast of the 'Celts of old', but it was hardly tactful to continually compare the present generation unfavourably. In addition, he was not above having a pop at the Celtic fans who did not turn out in sufficient numbers to support the club, something that caused a great deal of resentment among the many fans who would think nothing, when they were out of work in the Depression, of walking to places like Motherwell and Airdrie to see their team and even using a bicycle to take them to Perth, Kilmarnock and Dundee.

There were of course reasons why Celtic's home crowds were dipping alarmingly. It was probably true that the Depression did affect the Catholic population more than other parts of society, given the Church of Scotland's repeated fears of the 'Catholic menace' and absurd worries of the 'purity of the Scottish race' – sentiments that were not too far removed from what was being said in Germany at the same time, and that Celtic supporters had less money to use to support their team, particularly when the fare at Parkhead was not too great, and was admitted to be inferior to what Maley used to expect from his famous 'Celts of old'.

Yet, this must not be misinterpreted as any sign that Celtic were finished as a force in Scottish football. Big games remained well attended. Both the Scottish Cup Finals against Motherwell in 1931 and 1933 attracted six figure crowds, and the 1931 replay with a 5.00 pm kick-off on a Wednesday night was only a tad short of the six figures. Celtic were still a great team, and their return to greatness was much awaited and longed for. All that was needed was someone to kick them out of their lethargy.

In this of course we can see a parallel with 30 years later when Jock Stein returned to the club in early 1965. It is not of course an exact parallel, for Napoleon would only be a trainer, and although he would have a great deal of say in the choosing of the team, this would have to be done with subtlety and gradually, whereas Stein demanded and got instant control. McMenemy had of course been working with

Partick Thistle, whereas Stein had been manager of Dunfermline and Hibs and had already achieved success. Nevertheless the return in McMenemy on 15 October 1934 was greeted with tremendous enthusiasm by the fans.

The appointment suited Maley. He had of course feared being 'retired' (as indeed would eventually happen in January 1940) and replaced by someone like his friend John 'Sailor' Hunter of Motherwell or ex-Celt Paddy Travers of Aberdeen, both of whom would have insisted on Maley being given a back seat. In this situation, Maley would have McMenemy, whom he trusted and liked, as his assistant, doing all that was required of him.

The job of 'coach' or 'trainer' or 'assistant manager' was what suited McMenemy. He remained all his days a humble, self-effacing and mild-mannered man. Such qualities must never be mistaken for weakness of character, for he was never likely to get pushed around either on the field or off it, but the limelight was not for him. He would have been happy and contented for Maley to accept all the plaudits (Maley of course positively courted publicity even in his old age) while Jimmy would stay in the background. Photographs of McMenemy are revealing – a small man sometimes wearing the cloth cap, sometimes standing with it in his hand. Rod Steiger would not have relished the role of this Napoleon!

Celtic's start to the 1934–35 season had been dismal with only four League wins out of thirteen starts, and a 1–2 defeat to Rangers in the Glasgow Cup semi-final where the game had been described as 'Celtic's spirit against Rangers' skill'. Most humiliating of all had been the Jimmy McGrory benefit game when Rangers, without trying too hard, one imagines, nevertheless beat Celtic 4–0 before only 8,000 fans on a wet Monday night. It was clear then, that Celtic were in a crisis mode when McMenemy came back.

Yet looking at the players, there did not seem to be all that much wrong. Peter McGonagle was an excellent left-back and there was nothing too much wrong with Joe Kennaway in goal, nor Bobby Hogg at right-back. In the forward line there was still the prolific McGrory, but the O'Donnell brothers frequently disappointed in spite of the 'O'Donnell Abu' song that resounded round Parkhead in their honour. And then there was Charlie Napier, the natty dresser who often seemed as it he would have been a fine music hall act with a boater and cane, but whose performances in the field were unpredictable. Once again a song in his honour 'Clap, clap hands, here comes Charlie' did not always bring out the best in him. Like two subsequent men of the same Christian name, Tully and Nicholas, form could be infuriating and inconsistent.

There was however one player that McMenemy took an instant liking to. This was a slightly built, shy young man from Cleland called Jimmy Delaney, who had broken into the team this season on the right wing and was already impressing with phrases like 'a heartening discovery' appearing in the newspapers about him. He was speedy, ('charging down the wing like the fire brigade' is one particularly vivid description of him) direct, knew when to cross, could cut inside, and as important as anything else, had the right attitude. McMenemy, of course, knew what a good right-winger looked like – he had played alongside Alec Bennett and Andy McAtee, and this youngster seemed to have all the qualities. Napoleon would pay particular attention to his development.

More of a problem centred on Malcolm MacDonald. Born in South Uist originally but now domiciled in Glasgow, Malky or 'Calum' did not seem to enjoy the full confidence of Maley, and there seemed to be a major question mark about what his best position was. He was versatile, something that made him a very handy man to have around in the event of injuries, but his main position tended to be centre-half. McMenemy wondered about that, for MacDonald seemed to be too good a player to be centre-half in the sense that he had a great deal of dribbling and passing skills, whereas McMenemy's concept of the centre-half position was based on what he had seen from Willie Loney and Peter Johnstone – robust players who tackled and barged hard, and who did not disdain, when required, the big ugly punt up the field.

It may have been coincidence but after McMenemy's arrival, Celtic went on a winning streak ended only by an unlucky reverse to Hibs at Easter Road on 15 December. Nevertheless the pattern was one of improvement and after a fine 4–2 win over Hearts on 29 December, Celtic were being talked about seriously for the first time in a few years as title contenders. This all fell apart however on New Year's Day at Ibrox when in a brutal game which saw Napier taken to hospital for all the second half and Delaney also injured, Rangers scraped home 2–1, the cause not being helped by McGonagle being sent off for bouncing the ball off Rangers centre-forward Jimmy Smith's head after a crude challenge on Joe Kennaway.

Further defeats made the League challenge difficult, and the Scottish Cup saw a comprehensive defeat by Aberdeen at Pittodrie, the black and golds winning 3–1. Thus McMenemy's first season was trainer was a trophyless one, but one in which the thoughtful McMenemy had seen enough to suggest to Maley several improvements. Over the summer, the transfer activity was significant. The two O'Donnell brothers went to Preston North End and Napier to Derby County. McMenemy may have been unhappy at seeing these three fine players on their way, but he had already thought of ways to deal with their loss.

In a move unusual for the times, Celtic signed an Englishmen from Queen's Park. He was the centre-half Willie Lyon, a commanding figure of a man who would in time become a great captain. This was a great move, and to what extent McMenemy was involved in it, no one can be sure, but McMenemy certainly saw Willie Loney in Willie Lyon, even to the extent of on one occasion when talking to a newspaper reporter saying in a Freudian slip 'Loney' when he meant 'Lyon'.

He also felt that Jimmy McGrory, although now ageing, was still capable of scoring far more goals than he had done the past few seasons. Who better to consult on this problem than the great Jimmy Quinn, still a regular attender at Parkhead? Maley, always a great admirer of Quinn, could not nevertheless ask his advice about McGrory, but Napoleon could. 'So Jimmy, how do we get more goals out of McGrory?' Quinn's answer was brutal and to the point, 'Nae secret about it, Nap. Just get the ba' tae him as often as ye can. That's what Crum and Delaney and Geatons hae tae dae. Just gie the ba' tae Jimmy!'

They certainly did that in 1935–36, and McGrory produced the goods. This season has been compared by some historians to the 2000–01 season in which for Jimmy McGrory, read Henrik Larsson. Those of us who recall the glorious treble of that year will have some sort of idea of what that season was like, with goals, some of them brilliant ones, galore.

Not only was there a great goal scorer in position, but there were also loads of brilliant players who could supply the goalscorer with the ball, and could score goals themselves when the goalscorer himself was marked out of the game. The defence was good, the midfield was good and the forward line of Delaney, Buchan, McGrory, Crum and Murphy was deservedly lauded to the skies.

McMenemy was a great help to the developing Delaney, as we have said, and during the season another great winger came through in the shape of Frank Murphy, to whom history has been less kind than it ought to have been for no other reason than that Delaney was slightly the better winger. To say that one was only slightly inferior to Delaney was no insult to Murphy, for Delaney was absolutely splendid – and Murphy was not far behind.

McMenemy's contributions to this team were two-fold. One was the major tactical one of interchanging. A feature of the great team in which McMenemy played was their ability to change position with Bennett suddenly coming through on the left when the defence expected him on the right, Somers appearing on the right wing, and often crucially and tellingly, Quinn and Loney changing position, taking advantage of their similarity in build and way of running to outfox the opposition.

McMenemy tried this out in training. There is a certain amount of evidence that Maley tut-tutted and disapproved but McMenemy shrugged his shoulders and said 'He would' and continued on his merry way knowing that 'The Boss', as he insisted Maley should be known as, would mellow if he saw the benefits of Celtic's fast, attractive football. McMenemy knew better than anyone that what Maley really wanted was success on the field, and Maley knew that a decade had now passed without Celtic winning the Scottish League Championship, something that was unthinkable to those who had watched 'the Celts of old', as Maley kept calling them.

McMenemy's other contribution was on the social side. Although fundamentally a shy man, there was a side to McMenemy that allowed him to take part in the high-jinks and pranks that inevitably go on in any football team. Maley was past this stage. Indeed several players found it hard to conceal their dislike for his brooding and depressive despotism which led him to issue some ridiculous edicts like trying to forbid players to drive motor cars, and not allowing them to play sports like tennis and cricket in the summer. Malky MacDonald was only one of several players who would admit openly that if he got on a Glasgow tram and saw Maley on the upper deck, he would pretend not to notice him and go to the lower deck. He would also stay on the tram one stage further on than Celtic Park and choose to walk an extra couple of hundred yards rather than share the company of Maley.

The problem was that Maley was still a giant of the Scottish game, and indeed his moods could be quite unpredictable. He would suddenly stop a player and ask very kindly of his mother or grandmother who had been ill. He knew the names of all the players' wives and how many children everyone had. He could sometimes barge into the dressing room after training and say nice things about their attitude or suddenly hold court about the evils of Hitler or Stalin. But he could equally be brusque, unpleasant and rude, as even great players like Delaney, Paterson and McGrory would find out.

In these circumstances, there needed to be someone like Napoleon. Sympathetic and helpful, always ready to listen and always ready with a quip or a joke to cheer everyone up. He was not the sort of man one could take the loan of – in any case, he was such a great figure in Celtic's history that respect was automatic – but he did have a lighter side. His commitment was total, and he spent long hours at Celtic Park, talking about football mainly, but he was sufficiently urbane to be able to discuss other things as well. Through his constant talking to the players, he was able to spot problems even before they surfaced and to deal with them adequately. He was a man about whom no one had a bad word to say, and his position was all the stronger because, although he was definitely a member of the management team, he was emphatically NOT 'the Boss'.

The result of all this was that Celtic had a very noticeable and very well-developed team spirit. Tantrums and wanting transfers were things that tended not to happen in season 1935–36. Napoleon went out of his way to make sure that the fringe players, like Willie Hughes and Willie Fagan, were made to feel part of the squad and the great success that it was having. Injuries in the autumn to Peter McGonagle and Malky MacDonald more or less ruled them out for the season, but McMenemy handled a difficult situation well when their replacements Jock Morrison and Frank Murphy proved such a success.

The success of the team in 1935–36 was phenomenal. The first game at Pittodrie was lost (Celtic seldom won there between the wars) but the next League loss was 14 December away to an incredulous Dunfermline Athletic at the then primitive East End Park, the cause of the Pars helped by the absence of both Delaney and McGrory. In between that, McGrory scored in almost every game that he played in, scoring three hat-tricks and four braces with Celtic clearly obeying the instruction of getting the ball to McGrory whenever they could. McGrory had also by the end of the calendar year of 1935 reached two landmarks, both at Parkhead in front of his adoring fans, beating the records of Steve Bloomer in October and then that of Hughie Ferguson on midwinter's day, 21 December – a diving header on a bone hard pitch on a misty day against Aberdeen to make him the greatest goalscorer of all time, but then again the Celtic fans knew that anyway!

Young Celtic fans said to their Dads
As Parkhead's mist hung hoary
You can keep your Santa Claus
I just want James McGrory!

The only fly in the ointment had been a defeat in the Glasgow Cup Final to Rangers, a bitter blow this one but there were excuses in that goalkeeper Joe Kennaway was taken off injured and replaced by Chick Geatons for a long spell of the game. It was nevertheless a disappointment because it seemed to indicate that the Rangers complex (whereby superior Celtic teams folded before Rangers ones, and Celtic fans of the early 1960s and early 1990s will identify with that) had not gone away entirely.

Indeed, early 1936 saw many hearts begin to flutter with two bad blows. New Year's Day saw Rangers at Parkhead and after a thrilling encounter which delighted all neutrals, Rangers won by the odd goal in seven. Then in two weeks in early February, all Celtic's great work seemed to be undone when Hearts beat them in the League 1–0 at Tynecastle with a Tommy Walker penalty and the saving by Jack Harkness of a well-placed Willie Lyon penalty, and worse followed the next week when Celtic unaccountably went down 1–2 to St Johnstone at Parkhead in the Scottish Cup.

There seemed to be no real reason for this defeat other than that the pitch was hard and that many Celtic players had an off day while the Perth Saints played above themselves in what was probably the best result in their history. 26,647 watched in sullen silence as Delaney, injured early on, failed to get into the game and McGrory looked a lot less sharp than he had been, and was suddenly beginning to look his age (he was now nearly 32).

Celtic now found themselves at the crossroads. The Scottish Cup and the Glasgow Cup had now gone but the Scottish League Championship was still possible. The League was being led by Aberdeen and hopes were high in the North that they could win the Championship for the first time ever, but the major problem, as everyone knew, was Rangers.

The problem was that Celtic had eleven games left to play but had used up all their fixtures against Aberdeen and Rangers. In such circumstances, all one can do is win all your own games, with as high a margin as possible to improve the goal average, and tellingly, to put as much pressure as possible on your opponents to make them 'crack'. This had happened in 1915 and 1919, and Jock Stein famously did this in 1968, but 32 years earlier the combination of Maley and McMenemy did the same in 1936.

Fortunately McGrory returned to the goal standard, as the phrase went, and the rest of the team remained remarkably free of injuries that spring. Kilmarnock, Clyde and Hibs all conceded four goals and Ayr United six, but the most significant result was the 5–0 defeat of Motherwell on 14 March. Hitler had helped himself to the Rhineland the previous week, to the alarm of Britain and France, but even his stormtroopers were hardly as fast as Jimmy McGrory who scored in the 65th, 66th and 67th minute and the legend of 'goal a minute James McGrory' was born.

But wait a bit, don't go so fast
We've left the star turn to the last
There in the pride o' a' his glory
Goal a minute, James McGrory!

The following week Celtic visited the potentially difficult ground of Dens Park, and this time it was Delaney who scored in the first minute before McGrory added another before half-time.

This was Championship winning stuff. Aberdeen had already cracked and Rangers were now showing every sign of doing the same, unable to keep pace with the phenomenal goalscoring record of McGrory. McMenemy, realising that his team was on the verge of a great and historic season, worked hard to keep all the players fit and well for each game, taking each game as it came, never underestimating the forthcoming opposition and generally exuding an air of calm. On match day, he would be seen on the touchline with his primitive equipment of smelling salts and a sponge bag, occasionally shouting a word of advice, but more often allowing the players to take charge of their own destiny.

Both he and Maley had total faith in the man in charge on the pitch, namely Willie Lyon. A born leader and soon overcoming any prejudice that there might have been of him being an Englishman, Lyon was himself a great centre-half, and like Billy McNeill of later years, was a man who radiated command and confidence, the confidence coming from his regular Thursday afternoon chats with Jimmy McMenemy of whom it was now said that what he didn't know about Scottish football could fit comfortably on the back of a sixpence.

A 6–0 thumping of Ayr United in which McGrory scored a hat-trick to reach 50 goals for the season but then missed a penalty that would have made it 51, more or less won the League for Celtic but it was the following week in a 3–1 win at McMenemy's old stamping ground of Firhill that the League was officially confirmed. It was 25 April, Maley's 68th birthday and Maley made much of that, but everyone knew that the real architect of the triumph was Jimmy McMenemy, the quiet unassuming man who like all great Celts, was just an ordinary man.

There was a postscript to this season, and one wonders what McMenemy made of it all. It was the Glasgow Charity Cup Final on 9 May between Celtic and Rangers before a crowd of 43,162 at Hampden. Well inside the last ten minutes, the game was locked at 2–2 but Rangers were ahead on corners, the method used to decide

The Championship winning side of 1935-36. McMenemy is now the trainer, seated on the front row on the left.

drawn games in that tournament. Delaney had already scored twice, and then with time running out, scored again to put Celtic ahead and give himself a hat-trick. Then he fed McGrory to 'mak siccar' at 4–2, and Celtic had won a great triumph, for in an exact parallel with the Scottish League, they had not won the Glasgow Charity Cup since 1926.

Delaney was naturally very proud of what he had done. His team mates lauded him and the sporting Rangers players congratulated him. McMenemy showed his delight, and said 'Well done', before Delaney met the looming presence of Maley. Maley made as if to pass him without saying anything, but Delaney said something along the lines of 'Did you like that, Boss?' Maley looked at him and growled to the hat-trick hero, 'Don't let that go to your head now, son!'
Such was the nature of Maley in 1936, and this was why McMenemy was such a foil to him. If Delaney had been hurt by this behaviour (no reason why he would have, for he had surely proved his point), McMenemy would have been there to say that that was exactly what the Boss was like, he didn't mean it, he had a nice side to him too, he was getting old or whatever emollient sentiments were required. McMenemy had also needed all his diplomatic skills a month earlier – and for something that was not primarily to do with Celtic.

This was the choosing of the Scotland team to play at Wembley on 4 April. By any standards, several Celtic players should have been in that team, and certainly the two Jimmys, Delaney and McGrory. Delaney had played well against Ireland and Wales in autumn 1935, and McGrory was scoring goals more or less when he wanted. He had never played for Scotland at Wembley and 1930, 1932 and 1934 had seen heavy defeats. On the other hand, when he played against England at Hampden in 1931 and 1933, he had scored on each occasion and Scotland had won. Surely this time?

When the team was announced, it was not only Celtic sympathisers who gasped in amazement – no Delaney, no McGrory, but a place was found for Johnny Crum. Crum was a good player, but his contribution to the Celtic cause in 1936 was minimal in comparison with those of Delaney and McGrory. Crum, although delighted to have this opportunity, was embarrassed by the omission of the two Jimmys. Indeed Crum's presence seemed to be little other than a sop to injured Celtic feelings.

The whole business was irrational, but sadly typical of the muddled thinking of the Scotland Selectors, men who tended to be blazer-wearing Directors of teams like Queen of the South, Clyde or Falkirk. They meant well but frankly knew little about the form of players other than those who had played for or against their own teams in recent weeks. There was probably no deliberate or conscious anti-Celtic prejudice involved, for some Rangers players were sometimes equally irrationally treated, but it was hard to convince the Celtic fans that the problem lay in incompetence rather than bigotry or even bribery.

None of this made McMenemy's task in the dressing room any easier. Quite a lot of the other players had strong feelings on this issue, and Crum was sometimes the unfair target of cruel remarks. McMenemy however was always around to defuse the situation, and he was helped by two things – one was the gentlemanly demeanour of both Delaney and McGrory who quite genuinely wished Scotland and Crum well (the result turned out to be a 1–1 draw), and the other was that the Celtic side simply kept winning!

Summer 1936 was spent in great enthusiasm for the new season. The financial depression was visibly lessening but the international situation kept looking more and more gloomy, and for Celtic supporters there was a cruel splitting of loyalties, when the Spanish

Civil War broke out in July. Franco and the Army had risen against the Republican government, and were supported by the Roman Catholic Church. Scotland, of course, was a highly unusual country in that the Roman Catholic population tended to support a left wing political party, the Labour Party. The Spanish Civil War exposed this contradiction, for the Church wanted its adherents to back Franco, but the natural inclinations of the Celtic support would have been to side with the legitimate left-wing government. Things became even more complicated when the Roman Catholic Church baffled its adherents by seeming quite happy to accept the support of Hitler's Germany and Mussolini's Italy!

But above all, there was the fear of a more general war. Some brave souls went to Spain to fight for the International Brigades thinking (correctly) that the big struggle was fast approaching in any case, but most people went around clutching at straws in the hope that there would not be another war. The sheer amount of men, not yet old, going around with one arm, one leg or blinded, was a powerful argument against the folly of hostilities. Far better, if the Germans had to be put in their place, was the way that Jesse Owens did the job at the Berlin Olympics (Hitler was far from pleased at a black man doing so well) or (closer to home) the way that Jimmy Delaney scored two goals for Scotland against Germany in October.

There would also be the problem of the new King. King George V had died in January, and was succeeded by Edward VIII, a headstrong but well-meaning young man with more than a small liking for the playboy lifestyle with fast cars and even faster women. Rumours began to circulate in autumn 1936 about his association with a disreputable American lady called Wallis Simpson. Having discreet sexual relations with such a woman could be turned a blind eye to, but he wanted to marry her and make her Queen. She failed the test on three counts – she was American, she was a commoner and she had been divorced twice. Eventually the King had to be told it was either her or the crown. By December, he was on his way, leaving the throne to his brother Bertie, the stammering, shy, introvert with the more confident Scottish wife.

There was therefore enough to be going on with when the football season started. Season 1936–37 was a slight disappointment compared with the one that went before and the one that came after, but there were some fine compensations, one in particular. There was no real excuse in terms of injuries. McGrory was out for a spell in the early part of the season, and Buchan, Delaney and Murphy all had the occasional absences, but one would have expected the fine Celtic team of the previous year to cope with this. Sadly inconsistency particularly after the turn of the year cost Celtic dear and the League went to Rangers again.

But no fault could be laid at McMenemy's door, and it was a sign of the returning prosperity at Celtic Park that McMenemy was given an assistant. This was none other than Joe Dodds, the great left-back of the Great War years and immediately after. He was a wholehearted and earnest player with the ability to attack on occasion and also to take free kicks. Curiously, he does not seem to have got the adulation from Celtic historians that his consistent play over a period of fifteen years deserved, and there is a certain amount of evidence that he was never one of Maley's favourites. Maley was extremely reluctant to grant him a benefit, and for the 1920–21 season allowed him to go to Cowdenbeath rather than give him a pay increase! Even in the famous photograph taken after the 1937 Scottish Cup Final, when the two goalscorers, Buchan and Crum are pictured beside Maley and the two greats of yesteryear Quinn and McMenemy, one would have expected Dodds to have been there as well, but there is no sign of Joe.

So why was he appointed? Perhaps Maley mellowed, but perhaps it was more likely that Maley's influence was now waning and that the opinion of McMenemy now counted for a little more with the Directors. For whatever reason, McMenemy and Dodds was a fine combination. Dodds was a little less sociable than Napoleon in that he did not have such a supply of jokes and stories, but his technical knowledge and expertise was second to none.

For Celtic, the 1937 season was redeemed by the winning of the Scottish Cup in epic fashion before a dangerously overcrowded Hampden Park which contained far more than the 146, 433 officially credited. Yet it might not have happened. 30 January 1937 saw Celtic drawn in the Scottish Cup at Ochilview, the tiny ground of Stenhousemuir, a team whose perpetual struggle for survival calls for admiration from even the sternest of hearts. The first half was goalless, but when McGrory eventually scored for Celtic in the 70th minute, it was expected that a goal fest would ensue. Not so. Charlie Howie carved his name into Stenhousemuir immortality by equalising, and then in the very last minute of the game, Jock Morrison, Celtic's left-back, appeared to handle in the box. McMenemy's heart missed a beat, but veteran referee Peter Craigmyle said no to the frenzied appeals of the Stenny men. Various Celtic sources – like Eck McNair (who had of course played for both teams) and Jimmy Delaney (injured and watching from the stand) said later that they thought it was a penalty.

It so happened that this turned out to be a particularly good day for Celtic because Rangers, who had won the Scottish Cup for the last three years, lost that day to Queen of the South, thus installing Celtic as clear favourites for the trophy. Stenhousemuir were disposed of in the replay without any great fuss, as indeed were Albion Rovers and East Fife in subsequent rounds.

Motherwell now awaited. Motherwell had of course been beaten by Celtic in the Scottish Cup Finals of 1931 and 1933, and were thirsting for revenge. Parkhead would probably have hosted a crowd of over 60,000 on 10 March, but for an unseasonal and anti-climactic fall of snow, which postponed the game and reduced the attendance to 36,259 (still massive for midweek) on the following Wednesday afternoon.

Here the inflence of McMenemy was seen on Willie Buchan. Buchan of course was having a fine season, and was an inside-right in the same mould as McMenemy himself had been. McMenemy had often taken him aside and told him to 'Try the unexpected, Willie'. He would do just that to devastating effect that day.

Things looked grim for Celtic when just after half-time, Motherwell went into a 4–2 lead after some breathtaking football from both sides. But Celtic fought back, and with Willie Lyon in inspirational form:

'There's surely no denyin'
That wi' captain Willie Lyon
We'll win the Scottish Cup once again'

Celtic surged forward. They were awarded a penalty in the 51st minute, Lyon himself took it and scored, and for the next half hour laid siege to the Motherwell goal. Shots were saved by goalkeeper McArthur, defenders got in the way of fierce net bound drives, crosses were cut out before they could reach the lurking McGrory, and in spite of the constant barrage from Celtic attackers, backed up by crescendoes of noise from the fans, the Motherwell defence refused to yield.

Then well within the last ten minutes, Willie Buchan got the ball about 25 yards from goal. Wingers Delaney and Murphy automatically began to find space for themselves, expecting the pass, but Willie remembered what McMenemy had said about the 'unexpected'. Seeing that the Motherwell defence had attenuated itself by pursuing Delaney and Murphy, Buchan decided to have a go himself, dribbling past one man, then another before more or less walking the ball into the back of the net to cause an explosion of noise and acclaim within Celtic Park.

Another 35,000 crowd came to the replay, this time at tight little Fir Park in Motherwell where the crowd was swaying dangerously at several points, and simply had to be allowed onto the running track, less than a yard from the touchline. Thousands more were locked outside, compelled to judge the progress of the game by the roar of the lucky ones inside. The size of the crowd did not surprise the Celtic party for the team bus had passed thousands of fans on the road, many of them walking all the way from Glasgow to Motherwell.

Such support deserves success, and they got it as Celtic won 2–1 after having been 0–1 down at half-time. 76,000 were then at the semi-final at Hampden against Clyde. Celtic won 2–0 thanks to a low McGrory diving header to finish off a Murphy cross, and then a slightly more fortuitous own-goal, but the talking point was mainly the huge attendances that Scottish football, Celtic in particular, was attracting.

There were of course reasons in that everyone was now more or less back in work with loads of overtime available in shipyards and factories as the country braced itself for what was now apparently inevitable. And therein lay the other reason. There was a certain determination to enjoy oneself as long as one could, and there were few more enjoyable spectacles than the sight of a Celtic team playing glorious football, not unlike in the years before the previous war. And what was there in common between these two teams of more than 20 years apart? Jimmy McMenemy!

149,407 saw the Scotland v England game on 17 April. Only a few less than that, 146,433, saw the Scottish Cup Final a week later between Celtic and Aberdeen, but those who were at both games insist that in fact there were more at the Scottish Cup Final, and indeed the crowd was put unofficially as high as 154,000. It took a lot to overawe McMenemy but the sheer size and volume of the crowd did that. The city of Aberdeen (it was their first ever Scottish Cup Final) seemed to have emptied itself and migrated southwards en masse that day, and the Celtic crowd was as huge as it always was for a Scottish Cup Final.

It was almost certainly to be McGrory's last Cup Final, and it would have been nice if he could have done what he did in 1925, 1931 and 1933 and scored, but it was not to be. Crum and Buchan scored Celtic's goals, and Celtic had won the Scottish Cup for the 15th time in 49 years of existence. McMenemy had been officially involved in seven of these Celtic triumphs, six as a player and now one as trainer, and of course his family had been further involved in another three of these Cup Finals, for his son John had played in 1927, 1931 and 1933, although the latter two occasions had been for the opposition! Little wonder that Jimmy always felt a special symbiosis between himself and the Scottish Cup!

The season ended with a little more icing on the cake in the shape of the Glasgow Charity Cup Final when once again another late fightback reversed a score of Queen's Park 3 Celtic 2 into a 4–3 win for McMenemy's men. He would however have been a lot less proud of his men on the night of Friday 30 April when in a meaningless end of season game at Motherwell, the team disgraced themselves. They were about to embark on an overnight sleeper to London to see the

English Cup Final between Sunderland and Preston North End, and it may be that a little 'demob happy' behaviour entered the squad, for the team went down to a 0–8 defeat in which injuries were only a partial excuse. Maley was furious and McMenemy upset for such lack of professionalism, but it did not matter a great deal and has been relegated to the most obscure of footnotes in Celtic history.

Season 1937–38 was always likely to be a very special year in the history of Celtic FC. Everyone was aware that the club had been formed in November 1887 and had played its first game in May 1888, and that therefore this was the Golden Jubilee of the club that was regarded, not without cause, as the most successful in the world. Willie Maley had of course been absolutely pivotal to all this. He had played in the first game, had won a Scottish Cup medal, two Scottish League medals and had been capped for Scotland. Then appointed 'manager' in 1897 (whatever that meant then) he had within ten years built up the greatest team on earth, then repeated the feat ten years after that, and now in his old age, had another fine team. He was indeed 'The Man Who Made Celtic'.

But he was now not far off his 70th birthday which he would celebrate in April 1938. It did seem a fine time for him to announce his retirement after 50 years of heavy and constantly intimate involvement with Celtic. It had been clear in the past few years that he was less active than he once was, that he had his days of 'black dog' depression, that he was unpredictable with his staff and players and of course that he was relying to a large extent on McMenemy and now Dodds as well to see to the actual running of the team.

So much was it taken for granted that he would indeed announce his retirement in summer 1938 that it was widely speculated upon who would be his successor. The favourite was Paddy Travers, currently Manager of Aberdeen. Travers had left Celtic because he had been replaced by Patsy Gallacher but he had a fine knowledge of the game and had made Aberdeen a respectable force in Scottish football and Pittodrie a place from where Celtic in particular found it very hard to dig out a victory. Other names were mentioned too in John 'Sailor' Hunter, Manager of Motherwell and a good friend of Willie Maley, or James Logan who had done so well with Raith Rovers in the early 1920s. But where did McMenemy fit in to all this?

McMenemy was aware that he lacked the 'gravitas' and the 'dignitas' to be a Manager. He was not the sort of man about whom it could be said that the whole atmosphere changed when he walked into a room. This could be said of Maley and Struth (and in later years, of course, Jock Stein and Alex Ferguson). It was said that even if you had your back to the door, you knew by the body language of everyone else that Maley had entered. But McMenemy was self-effacing, did not automatically command your attention and was almost insignificance in appearance.

Yet against that, there was a football brain second to none. He had the same love of Celtic and indeed the same detailed knowledge of the special requirements of this special club, he could assess a situation, a player and a ground as well as anyone. His contribution in his lengthy playing career from 1902 to 1922 had been outstanding (arguably more than anyone else) but, crucially, he had never been captain, apart from the odd occasion with injuries etc. He was not a leader of men. He was an adviser, a confidant, a mentor, a motivator, an encourager and a shoulder to cry on – all of these things – but he was not necessarily a leader. The choice of headgear usually gave it away. Maley always wore his imposing homburg hat, Napoleon wore the ubiquitous Scottish working man's bonnet.

All these considerations however would wait until summer 1938. Maley would not countenance any sort of stepping back before then.

There was a League Championship to be won, and the players were there to do it. But there were two significant departures in the autumn of 1937, a time when the team never really seemed to be settled. They disappointed their fans by losing twice to Rangers, once in the Scottish League and once in the Glasgow Cup. McGrory played what turned out to be his last game against Queen's Park on 16 October 1937. Fittingly he scored, but was injured and missed the next few games before it became apparent that he was not going to recover from this one. In December came the announcement that he would be taking over as Manager at Kilmarnock.

This was disappointing but perhaps inevitable. McGrory was now old for a centre-forward and had been on the receiving end of many knocks in his long career of nearly 15 years at Celtic Park. McGrory left with the best wishes of all concerned, but he would play an important part in the fortunes of Celtic that season, as we shall discover.

The other departure caused far more controversy. It was the transfer of Willie Buchan (according to what he himself said, he was simply told by Maley that he was 'going' and had little say in the matter) for £10,000 to Blackpool in October 1937. The fans were incensed, for there was no more popular player than Buchan, and it seemed that Celtic had returned once again to their mindset of money being more important that players on the park. In fact, it was not a bad piece of business, and McMenemy may have suggested it. He was certainly shrewd enough to have done so.

Celtic had Malky MacDonald, a man who had played all over the team for the past few years but had never really commanded any position. McMenemy however knew a player when he saw one and he certainly knew an inside-right when he saw one. MacDonald was in no way an inferior of Buchan (or anyone else) and when Blackpool, who had long admired Buchan, offered the king's ransom of £10,000 it seemed folly to turn it down when a ready made replacement was available.

McDonald very soon won over any doubters that he might have had, and with McGrory now out of the picture the forward line moved almost seamlessly from Delaney, Buchan, McGrory, Crum and Murphy to Delaney, MacDonald, Crum, Divers and Murphy, for McMenemy had also seen a considerable amount of talent in John Divers. In fact, he had been told about him often enough, for John was the nephew of McMenemy's old colleague Patsy Gallacher! Patsy had frequently asked Napoleon when his nephew was going to get a game!

The new team clicked almost immediately and an impressive unbeaten run was built up over the winter. It had included a Christmas Day massacre of a poor Kilmarnock side, being managed for the first time by no less a person than Jimmy McGrory! Jimmy was, of course, given a great welcome by the Parkhead crowd who then settled down to see an 8–0 hammering with Maley determined that, McGrory or no McGrory, there would be no easing up. New Year's Day saw an even better result for Celtic as Rangers were defeated 3–0 in a very one-sided Old Firm game in which both Crum and MacDonald starred. The crowd was given as 92,000 and is frequently said to be the highest ever crowd at Celtic Park. Evidence, in fact, suggests that the crowd may have been a little less that that, for *The Glasgow Herald* states '83,500 with more than 10,000 turned away', but it was still a huge attendance with the exuberant crowd invading the field at the end to congratulate their heroes.

Celtic's triumphant winter continued. Another huge crowd saw them beat Hearts at Tynecastle in January, a feature of this game being the amount of supporters who arrived in Edinburgh overnight (some having walked or having commandeered a lorry) and began to queue outside the ground from about six or seven in the morning and being seen to drink bottles of milk and eat rolls while the good ladies of the Gorgie Road wondered why their normal breakfast materials had not been delivered!

The following week in the Scottish Cup, Cathkin Park was stretched to breaking point to see Celtic beat Third Lanark. February was similarly triumphant, and Celtic fans were able to revel in the achievements of their team and to pay little attention to Hitler's attempts to 'persuade' Austria to join a Greater Germany. In so far as they did notice this major threat to world peace, they could ask the same question about why Ulster should not be coerced into joining the 'real' Ireland. In the meantime, Spain's agony continued as Great Britain, France and the United States turned their backs on a democratic country being ripped apart by Fascist beasts.

Early March however brought Celtic up with a start. In the Scottish Cup, Kilmarnock came to Celtic Park as 39,528 turned up to see what they thought would be a repeat of the Christmas Day massacre. They were in for a shock. In the first place Celtic ran out in green shirts with white sleeves (what would become after the war the recognised 'Hibs' strip!) and playing very badly were two goals down at half-time to a very fine Kilmarnock side who had clearly improved immensely under McGrory.

Half-time saw Parkhead in an eerie, uncomprehending silence and McMenemy had to work hard to gee up the players who were not used to being behind and indeed to being outplayed as they clearly were on this occasion. Chick Geatons was out, and his deputy Matt Lynch was struggling, but that was no excuse, for this Celtic team really should have beaten Kilmarnock. The team did rally, and Malky MacDonald converted a penalty within the last 15 minutes, but in spite of fanatical encouragement, the equaliser and the lifeline of a replay simply did not come. Full-time saw Celtic leave the field dispirited and defeated.

The aftermath was significant. Maley, for all his pious protestation in the past that, 'It is our proud boast that we can taste the fruits of victory in the same spirit as the bitterness of defeat' pointedly ignored McGrory when Jimmy sought him out after the game. McGrory was upset at this boorish treatment, and it was left to McMenemy to offer congratulations. From now on, Maley would underplay McGrory's contribution to Celtic, often doing it subtley and indirectly by praising Jimmy Quinn whom he would loudly declare to the the best 'centre-forward of them all'. But there was another side-effect as well. It may have been this result that persuaded the Celtic Directors seven years later at the end of the Second World War in 1945 that McGrory would be a suitable man to be the Manager of Celtic. In this, they made a huge misjudgement.

With Maley now lapsing once again into brooding silence occasionally making incomprehensible statements about 'betrayal' and not doing very much at all to help the team, it was up to McMenemy to pick up the pieces. This he did admirably, but there were further stutters in the shape of a couple of draws before an appalling defeat at Falkirk (admittedly without Delaney) which raised serious questions in the minds of some supporters about the attitude of certain players. But McMenemy once again said his usual 'Keep the Heid, Celtic' and two important wins over the Easter Weekend against Dundee (Dens Park on the Saturday, Celtic Park on the Monday) were instrumental in seeing Celtic home. The League was won for the nineteenth time on 23 April when two goals from Crum and one from Delaney were enough to see off St Mirren at Love Street and deliver the title to the grumpy old man two days before his 70th birthday.

But everyone knew who had been running the show. Indeed there was a conscious attempt at parody of the *Oh Dear What Can The Matter Be* song of old, when 'two goals from Quinn and one from McMenemy' could be easily replaced by 'two goals from Crum and one from Delaney'. Napoleon would smile to himself when he heard them singing that song.

There was of course a great deal more to come in that summer of 1938. In the first place the Glasgow Charity Cup was picked up for the third year in a row, this time in a very easy 2–0 win over Rangers before 40,000 at Hampden, and then of course came the Empire Exhibition Trophy which proved that Celtic were the best in Britain – and of course Crum's impromptu Highland Fling after the winning goal against Everton has passed into legend. Once again, McMenemy planned it all, coping admirably with the injuries to MacDonald and Delaney in the earlier games against Sunderland and Hearts and persuading his players not to be overawed by Everton in the Final. The famous cry of 'Fetch a polis man – Everton's getting murdered' may well have originated in the dressing room from McMenemy.

Even Maley relaxed and smiled. He came into the dressing room and while all his players were still naked in their bath told them that they had 'wiped the sting of the defeat by Kilmarnock in the Scottish Cup clean away'. They most certainly had, but it was clear what had been seething inside Maley.

A few days later came the Centenary Dinner at the Grosvenor Hotel. Maley was of course the hero of the hour, and made the most of all the attention while the modest McMenemy sat beside his old colleagues Loney and Quinn. Maley talked at length about what Celtic had done and finished up with a statement to the effect that 'the club has been my very life and without it, my existence would be empty indeed' Such sentiments were much appreciated by his audience, but crucially, he did not do what was expected of him – to announce his retirement. It would have been better if he had.

Celtic now fell away in an astonishingly disappointing way for their fans. Oddly enough this would be repeated exactly fifty years later when after a very successful Centenary season in 1988, McNeill's fine side simply imploded after a 1–5 beating at Ibrox and from then on resembled a rabbit transfixed in the glare of the Ibrox motor car, plunging their supporters into untold depths of despair and eventually after several years of the most excruciating pain, bringing about a major regime change.

The parallels between 1938 and 1988 are not exact of course, but in some ways there was an eerie similarity, the most obvious facet of which was complacency and resting on laurels. In 1938 Celtic had reached their apogee. They were the best team and best-supported team in Great Britain, and Maley had achieved what he had always wanted to achieve since the day in 1892 when he looked out of the horse-drawn charabanc returning from the first ever Scottish Cup win to see the impoverished and ill-clad urchins with a smile on their face, because 'our bhoys had won the Cup'.

But life moves on and is unforgiving to those who do not move with it. It is however only fair to see this season of 1938–39 in the context of the world. When the season opened in August, the odds would have been on war before Christmas as Hitler, with Austria already in the bag, made designs on the new country called Czechoslovakia. Indeed it was only the diplomatic skills or the craven cowardice (depending on one's 'take') of British Prime Minister Neville Chamberlain in September 1938 which prevented war a year earlier than it did in fact happen.

Chamberlain was not a man who would naturally be beloved of the Celtic faithful. A stiff, unpleasant man, permanently wearing dickie collars and lacking even the charisma of other Tories like Eden and Churchill, he did however have one moment of glory when he staved off war at Munich in late September. Contrary to what later historians with the benefit of hindsight maintain, the 'betrayal' of Munich was in fact very popular with the people, not least the Celtic fans who went to Albion Rovers on 1 October 1938 to see an 8–1 victory, and who looked at the thousands of disabled war veterans from twenty years ago and thanked God that it was not going to happen again – as it seemed.

There was no inkling in the early weeks of the season that Celtic were going to blow up. The season opened with a 9–1 win over Jimmy McGrory's Kilmarnock, a result that seems to have brought great joy to Willie Maley. And then early September saw an impressive 5–1 win over Hearts at Tynecastle, once again dangerously overcrowded, before 74,500 saw Celtic put Rangers to the sword to the tune of 6–2 with MacDonald and Delaney both on song. By the middle of October, Delaney, Geatons and Crum had scored the goals which beat Clyde and brought the Glasgow Cup back to Celtic Park for the first time since 1930.

It was only in the winter that things began to go wrong. Games that should have been won were drawn, and Celtic began to blame referees and heavy ground for their own inadequacies. There was some substance in their complaint about heavy grounds for most of their star players like Delaney and Crum were slightly built and less effective than on firmer pitches, but that should have been counter-acted at an earlier stage than it was, and then on 23 November it was announced that Malky MacDonald, arguably the best player at Parkhead at the time, had appendicitis. He would be out until January, by which time the damage had been done.

Divers, Crum and Delaney were all out for spells as well, the 'festive' period was anything but. The 1–3 defeat at Pittodrie was in the tradition of Celtic's poor showings there, then they could only draw with Hearts at Parkhead on Hogmanay before they lost narrowly and unluckily to Rangers on 2 January at Ibrox. So many were the injuries now that McMenemy could not cope with them all, and the team sent out to play Queen's Park on 3 January was barely recognisable with only five first team regulars. Predictably they lost 0–1 and then travelled to Kirkcaldy to surrender 0–4 to a Raith Rovers side which could hardly believe their luck.

The League was now gone, and it was a clear case of the team not having enough quality reserves to cover for injuries. To some extent McMenemy is to blame for this, but the real mistake was made in summer 1938 when Celtic stood still and did not bring in fresh talent. The same mistake was made in 1988. It was also now obvious that Maley was being seen even less and less at Celtic Park, and that Napoleon was in charge. The question was also being asked if the lovable Jimmy was up to the job.

The rest of the season was a slight improvement, albeit once again bedevilled by injuries and inconsistencies. The Scottish Cup saw trips to places like Burntisland and Montrose before yet another trip to an overcrowded Tynecastle. 50,709 saw Celtic score twice early on through Delaney and MacDonald before Hearts fought back and equalised with the last kick of the game. This meant a Wednesday afternoon replay at Celtic Park at which we are told that an extraordinary 80,840 attended, including an trainload of supporters who disgorged on the railway line at the west end of the ground when the train was stopped illegally by a sympathetic driver!

This amazing crowd (if it was as large as that) crammed into Parkhead to see a game that went to extra-time before John Divers resolved the issue. Unfortunately it was all in vain for in the quarter-final, before an all-ticket crowd at Fir Park, Motherwell gained a little revenge for their several Scottish Cup heartbreaks at the hands of Celtic, and Celtic's last peace time season came to an end with a whimper, especially when Jimmy Delaney suffered a horrendous arm break in a meaningless game against Arbroath at Celtic Park.

War of course came on 3 September 1939. Unlike in 1914 when it all happened unexpectedly, this one had been seen a long way away on the horizon. Indeed credit, as we have indicated, should be given to Britain's politicians for delaying it. It might well have happened a year earlier. As it was, all the 1938–39 season was played under the shadow of imminent war and when in spring 1939, Hitler without any attempt at negotiation, simply helped himself to all of Czechoslovakia, war was certain. It was only a question of when.

Football was immediately closed down, only to be opened up again in a limited form. No Internationals, Scottish Cup or Scottish League were allowed, but the two Glasgow Cups were still permitted and the Scottish League was replaced by the Western Regional League. Players' conditions were strictly controlled, and every player had to have a full time war-related job. Conscription was, of course, in force and players could be taken away, sometimes at short notice.

Maley, now over 71, simply could not cope with all this. He had done so well in the previous war when he was younger and more active, but as the team had been struggling in 1938–39 in any case, the situation was just too much for him. By Christmas, Celtic had won only two games, had drawn another two and lost five. This was too much, and Maley's 'retirement' was announced on New Year's Day.

The new Manager was the ex-captain Jimmy McStay. McMenemy was kept on, the clear implication being that he was not to be considered for the job as Manager. McMenemy was almost 60, but age need not have been a consideration, although there was an uncomfortable reminder of his own mortality early in the New Year of 1940 when it was announced that Napoleon's old friend and comrade Alec Bennett had passed on. McMenemy was of course heart-broken by this, and probably very disappointed at not getting the Celtic job at least for the duration of the war, but he stayed on for the sake of continuity – at least for the time being – with a good grace.

Not so Maley. Ten long years would pass before he was seen back again at the ground he loved so much, and which was so much part of his identity, He would go to Cathkin, Hampden and Ibrox and was made very welcome at all three locations, but the rift between himself and the Celtic Directors was a serious one, all apparently stemming from an argument about an honorarium and income tax, but its roots were a lot deeper than that.

McMenemy did not last much longer. He stayed on the bench the rest of the season, a dreadful one, but then suddenly at the Glasgow Charity Cup semi-final against Third Lanark on 18 May 1940 he did not appear in his usual place on the bench. The trainer's duties were done by Chick Geatons (who was still a registered player but not playing that day) but no official statement was made. Celtic won the game, but the Charity Cup Final against Rangers on 22 May (a humiliating defeat) still saw no McMenemy. McMenemy himself said nothing – he was not the sort of man who would sell his story to the newspapers, and in any case world circumstances meant that far more important things than who Celtic's trainer was dominated everyone's interest.

Hitler had invaded the Low Countries on 10 May (the same day as Churchill had been appointed Prime Minister of Great Britain), a few days after that, Rotterdam was obliterated in an example of 'saturation bombing' and very soon the British Army would be in headlong rout to Dunkirk. Such things were more important than whether Napoleon had or had not effectively left the club's employ. The circumstances of his departure – sacking, resignation, retirement? – are not known, but when the new season opened in August 1940, Alex Dowdells was Celtic's trainer, while McMenemy, still a few months short of his 60th birthday and therefore young enough to work, found a job in a war-related industry.

Chapter 8

THE FOOTBALLING FAMILY

Napoleon had three footballing sons. The least successful of the three, Frank is credited with having played for Burnbank, Hamilton Academical, St Cuthbert's, Hamilton Academical again, Nithsdale Wanderers, Airdrieonians, Northampton Town and Crystal Palace, John played for a variety of junior teams, then Celtic and Motherwell winning honours with both teams and then finishing his career with Partick Thistle and St Mirren, and Harry, the youngest of the three played six years with Newcastle United before finishing his career with Dundee.

John was an inside-right, like his father, and had played for both St Anthony's and St Roch's (the springboards of Tommy McInally and Jimmy McGrory respectively) before joining Celtic on 1 December 1925. He was described in junior circles as 'never showy, but valuable'. In some ways, given his family connections, it was indeed the 'only team he wanted to play for', but it was not necessary the wisest of choices for the youngster to make, for being the son of Napoleon did carry with it a certain amount of baggage. He would have had to be good to live up to the expectations engendered by his illustrious father.

Father and son combinations don't always work well at the same football team. Celtic have had two Gordon Marshalls playing in goal for them, and two John Divers in the forward line, and one or two others, but it is never easy for a son to do the same as his father. Yet, one would have imagined that Napoleon, his lengthy playing career now finished, would have been very happy to see young John don the green and white.

It would be some time however before he could break through to the first team. The 1925–26 team was a superb Celtic side which won the League Championship with a degree of ease and might have won the Scottish Cup as well had it not been for a degree of complacency which crept into the play and allowed St Mirren to record an unlikely triumph in the Final.

John would have been disappointed at not breaking through into the first team that season but as the inside-forwards were the ever-ready and reliable Alec Thomson, and the charismatic, will o' the wisp Tommy McInally, openings for a youngster were unlikely. He might have been on the point of despair when the following season was coming to its end and he still had not made his first team debut (although he had played once or twice on loan for Motherwell), but then fame and glory were suddenly thrust upon him.

It all came about when Tommy McInally broke his nose at Tynecastle on the Wednesday night of 30 March 1927. McMenemy must have hoped for his chance in the game against Dunfermline on the following Saturday, but the opportunity went instead to Frank Doyle who turned out to be far from impressive in Celtic's narrow 2–1 victory. But that Saturday 2 April saw momentous and distressing events a mile away at Hampden, for Scotland lost their first ever game at that ground since it opened in 1903 in a 1–2 defeat to England.

This defeat plunged the whole country into a frenzy of mourning and introspection the likes of which would not be seen again until Argentina in 1978. Scotland simply did not lose to England in those days, and scapegoats had to be found. Falkirk's left-back Bob Thomson had, by all accounts had a poor game and was universally blamed for the loss of England's winning goal but right-back Willie McStay, captain of Celtic and Scotland, did not help matters at all by stating that 'if Hutton or Hilley had partnered me at full-back, Scotland would not have lost'.

This was a little unfair, and was certainly tactless, causing gratuitous offence to a team mate, and was much resented in Falkirk. In addition, Celtic had already put Falkirk (Patsy Gallacher and all) out of the Scottish Cup, and it was generally agreed that the town of Falkirk and Celtic had never had a good relationship at the best of times. Now Celtic travelled to Falkirk on the Wednesday night immediately after the International to play a team seething with hatred and a desire for revenge. This was the game in which John McMenemy made his Celtic debut!

The pitch was hard and bumpy, the crowd were nasty and meaty challenges were dished out by a few brutal defenders. McStay was constantly barracked, and on the half-hour mark, McGrory was unceremoniously bundled to the ground by a brutal challenge and he suffered two broken ribs, enough to put him out of the rest of the season. Without McGrory and McInally (still out with his broken nose) Celtic struggled and the game simply passed poor John McMenemy by as Falkirk, with Patsy Gallacher giving every impression that he was making a point to Celtic, won 4–1.

Rather to his surprise and delight, one feels, McMenemy retained his position for the next game at Tannadice Park against bottom of the table Dundee United. It was a dreadful game with appalling defending on both sides producing a 3–3 draw, but McMenemy did manage to score one of the goals to keep him in contention for a place in next week's Scottish Cup Final against Second Division East Fife.

It was looked upon as a fairly easy task – so much so that Maley dismissed out of hand any suggestion from the players that they could be paid an extra bonus 'Get out and bring me back that Cup!' he peremptorily told his captain Willie McStay, but without McGrory what could he do for a centre-forward? Frankly, none of the deputies impressed, so Maley decided to put Tommy McInally back in the centre (where he had played at the beginning of the decade) and bring in John McMenemy at inside-left.

Whether he consulted John's father about this move is not clear, but John appeared at Hampden that day not knowing whether or not he would be playing. He was given the nod about half an hour before kick-off. This was only his third game for Celtic and was before a crowd of nearly 80,000 who were making a fair noise, it is hardly surprising that the youngster had an attack of nerves, finding it very difficult to lace his boots. Maley, not always the most tactful or sympathetic of men, turned to him and asked him why he was shaking. 'It's the ones in the other dressing room who should be shaking! It is an honour and a privilege to wear that green and white jersey! Your father did it often enough! Go and prove yourself worthy!' This low tolerance of nerves was of course a Celtic characteristic for legend has it that Jimmy Quinn once slapped the face of Davie Hamilton before a Cup Final when the frail Hamilton was showing signs of being nervous!

Young McMenemy need not have worried. Although East Fife scored first, they then immediately conceded an own goal, and from them on Tommy McInally took over. The 3–1 scoreline should have been a lot more, but Tommy eased up on them. Newspaper reports don't mention McMenemy very much, other than occasionally talking about 'good work from all the forwards'. The one exception is Waverley the much respected correspondent of *The Daily Record* who says:

Now for the baby of the forward line. I refer to John McMenemy, a worthy son of a worthy sire – the football 'Napoleon' I mean. This tall twenty-years old lad, if not so fast as he might be and may become, is a quick-thinker. He seems to have the real football brain – probably acquired through heredity.

After he had played himself in, 'Young Mac' brought the ball down like a master, and in that same movement, I might say, sent it on beautifully and almost invariably with accuracy to the man best placed to receive it. McMenemy minor seemed to have his mind made up as to what he would do with the ball before it was actually his.

What he lacked was punch, but this may come with pace – as he gets older. This McMenemy boy made a first-rate debut.

In truth, it was a dull final, but the McMenemy family had now won eight Scottish Cup medals. In a less happy game on the following Monday Celtic lost 0–1 to Rangers in a League match.

That really was as good as it got for John McMenemy at Celtic Park. He was not in the team on a regular basis in season 1927–28.

He was drafted in to cover for McInally's suspensions and tantrums (and there was a fair amount of that as far as Tommy was concerned that season) but he hated that role and probably, being a level headed young man, did suffer from the general instability brought to the club by McInally. Maley, who was not always so tolerant of wayward behaviour, did seem to minimise the follies of McInally, and allowed him back into the fold in the spring. As a result a possible double was thrown away, the Cup disastrously so in a 0–4 defeat by Rangers in the Scottish Cup Final.

John McMenemy was still struggling to find a place in the team the following season, when Motherwell expressed an interest. Manager John 'Sailor' Hunter had long been a fan of John's and by the end of October, Celtic, on yet another economy drive, were glad to let John go, even to a rival team. He had never really made it at Parkhead, and certainly was irked by the constant comparison with his father, but in winning a Scottish Cup medal in 1927, he does possess his own little corner of Celtic history. He was described by *The Glasgow Observer* as 'methodical, some say slow, not as astute as Alec Thomson, but with a powerful shot. He is often sluggish'.

At Motherwell, it was a new lease of life. Motherwell were a team on the up, and although progress was slow at the start for the still young John McMenemy, by the early 1930s they were a superb side, well moulded and led by the 'Sailor', a man who had earned that nickname in his playing days for Dundee some twenty years earlier not because of any service in the Royal or Merchant Navies, but rather because of his rolling way of walking which reminded supporters of sailors coming on shore and regaining their 'land legs'. He had been a fine player for Liverpool and Dundee, and now was producing a team which would challenge Celtic and Rangers.

For a provincial side to do this, there really must be loads of good players around, and good football must be played. Indeed it was at Fir Park in the early 1930s, in many ways similar to the way that Dundee played some 30 years later to win the League Championship of 1962. Motherwell won the League Championship in 1932, thus becoming the only non-Old Firm team to do so between Third Lanark in 1904 and Hibs in 1948 – a remarkable statistic, very damning to Scottish football and saying very little for the likes of Hearts or Aberdeen.

It was John's fortune to be part of the mighty forward line of Murdoch, McMenemy, McFadyen, Stevenson and Ferrier, still talked about in the Steel town to this day. For John McMenemy, this was an excellent team to be part of, and there seems little doubt that had he played for Celtic as well as he did for Motherwell, he would indeed be mentioned in the same breath as his illustrious sire. Willie McFadyen scored 52 goals in the season that they won the League, thus putting him in the same bracket as McGrory (however blasphemous that may sound!) and so many of his goals came from the tireless work of McMenemy, whose position was normally a little behind the other four forwards. Yet when the opposition least expected it, he could come forward and score as well.

McMenemy was possibly a shade less tricky than his father, but he was a good passer, had a fine turn of speed and, crucially, was always prepared to work hard and forage for the ball when it did not come to him automatically. He possibly felt that he had a point to prove to those in charge at Celtic Park, for he felt that he had not been given enough of a chance, and like his father, he was a level headed young man. He had certainly seen in the example of Tommy McInally that no matter how talented a player one is, application, hard work and attitude are of crucial importance as well.

At Motherwell too he found three great advantages. One was that he was not constantly compared to his father and referred to as 'Napoleon's son', another was that the Manager was far more amenable. Maley could be charming, but he was equally likely to be boorish and insensitive to young players, whereas 'Sailor', although not without a crusty and ruthless streak, was far more relaxed with his players and infinitely more approachable. And of course the third advantage of playing for Motherwell was that one was allowed an occasional bad game without having the supporters on one's back. Frankly, Celtic fans were not always tolerant of youngsters learning their trade. Success was demanded instantly – and of course at this era of history was not always forthcoming.

John McMenemy would win three caps for the Scottish League and one for the full Scotland team, with his performance in the 4–3 defeat of the English League on 7 November at Celtic Park particularly to be commended as he played well with Jimmy McGrory and Bob McPhail to produce the goals in a very good game of football much enjoyed by a crowd of 51,000. His one full cap came against Wales in October 1933 (in curious family circumstances, as we shall discover) but he can count himself unfortunate not to have been chosen for the Wembley International of 1932. Perhaps it was as well that he wasn't, for it was a massive Scottish defeat.

The Scottish Cup Finals of 1931 and 1933 between Celtic and Motherwell have now passed into folklore with the 1931 Final in particular a collector's item of stories and legends. We might care to pause and reflect on how it affected the McMenemy family. John had scored one of Motherwell's early goals, admittedly a softish one involving a deflection off McStay's leg and now with the second half well advanced, his team were 2–0 up, as the ever more desperate

Celtic side mounted attack after attack but with McMenemy back helping the defence, sometimes leaving Willie McFadyen, on his own up front, the punchless Celtic inside men were failing to get the ball to McGrory.

With everyone in the ground looking up at the big clock on the South Stand, John must have felt that a Cup winners' medal was getting closer, and that although he would not have been the first player to win a Scottish Cup medal with two separate clubs, certainly the McMenemy family, father and son, each to have achieved this feat would surely be something that would attract attention all over the world.

But then McGrory did score – but too late surely to affect the result. The Motherwell supporters certainly thought so with their American style razzamataz chants of 'Give us an M' and then someone would hold up the letter 'M', 'Give us an O' and someone standing beside him would hold up an 'O' and so on, while the Celtic fans, their banners drooping along with their faces, beginning to trudge up the high terracing and the long, broken-hearted trek home as some of the Celtic Directors in the stand were preparing to offer their congratulations to their Motherwell counterparts.

But then Bertie Thomson on the ball on the right wing under the Hampden stand, the hopeful punt, the centre-half rising to deal with it before McGrory got near, the momentary lapse of concentration, the ball skidding off the side of his head, the own-goal, the half-empty Celtic end behind the goal erupting in joy, and poor Alan Craig lying pummelling the ground as even Jimmy McGrory and referee Peter Craigmyle attempted to comfort him.

John knew then that the game was up, and that Celtic would win the replay. How he envied the crowd behind that goal as they belted out their anthems about 'Erin's Green Valleys' and 'We don't give a damn for no Orange man' with little boys carried shoulder high and holding banners with harps and shamrocks on them! If he had not been a professional football player, he would undeniably have been among them… as it was, he sunk to his knees in the despair that only the cruellest twist of the knife of fortune can bring.

And how would old Jimmy have felt? He had talked in newspapers about split loyalties, but anyone who has ever loved the Celtic will tell you, there is no going back. You discover in moments like this who you really love, and although there was a great deal of family loyalty and genuine disappointment for his son, his predominant emotion would have been joy that his team were still in the Scottish Cup. On Wednesday night when they finished the job, he would have felt the same, but he would also have been glad to read *The Daily Record* describing John as 'the best of the inside-forwards'.

But Napoleon would have been very genuinely proud of John the following year, the 'annus mirabilis' of Motherwell history when the team amassed 66 points and McFadyen scored 52 goals, and the League Championship was won. 1932 was a great year for the McMenemys with John winning the Scottish League and younger brother Harry winning the English Cup with Newcastle United. And how Jimmy must have wished that he could have been in two places at once on the afternoon of 12 March 1932!

Motherwell were at Celtic Park in a game which would perhaps indicate whether they really were Championship winning material or not. Celtic had not recovered from the death of John Thomson the previous September and had been dealt a further blow with the news that Peter Scarff was suffering from pulmonary tuberculosis (a fatal condition in the 1930s). They were having a poor season, not really in contention for the League Championship and

Motherwell had already put them out of the Scottish Cup at an earlier stage. Yet for Motherwell, a trip to Celtic Park was always a big occasion. Jimmy McMenemy would probably have been happy to support Motherwell on this occasion, for Motherwell's only real challengers for the Championship were Rangers!

But he wasn't there, for we know that he was invited to Huddersfield to see the English Cup semi-final between Newcastle and Chelsea as a guest of Newcastle United, for his other son Harry was playing for Newcastle. As it turned out, John played magnificently in Motherwell's 4–2 defeat of the dysfunctional Celtic, a result that did indeed mark Motherwell out as champions, for they had lost only two games in the League that season – to Kilmarnock in August and to Rangers on the day after Christmas. When Rangers beat them again, this time in the Scottish Cup the week before they played Celtic, there had been fears that they might implode (as provincial sides often do) but Motherwell's nerve held firm and the title was clinched on 23 April when with Motherwell not playing, Rangers failed to beat Clyde and could therefore not catch the 'Well. The town of Motherwell celebrated with all the enthusiasm that one would expect from a provincial town that has just beat the big city boys, and the celebrations were something that John would carry with him until his death in 1982.

In fact 23 April 1932 was a glorious day for the McMenemy family for it was the day of the English Cup Final of Newcastle United v. Arsenal, and Harry was playing at inside-left for the Geordies. Scottish people had every cause to support Newcastle, for not only are they physically the closest English team to Scotland but they had on this occasion no fewer than six Scotsmen in their side and their Manager was Andy Cunningham, the ex-

Rangers inside-right. It is a shame that this game was defined and continues to be defined by the 'over-the-line' incident of Newcastle's equaliser. Newsreel pictures show conclusively that Jimmy Richardson and the ball were clearly over the deadball-line when he crossed for Jack Allen to score Newcastle's equaliser.

Regrettably this incident tends to minimise the part played by men like McMenemy (by some distance the youngest of the 22) in Newcastle's great triumph which meant so much the the poverty-stricken people of the North East – the area of the racing pigeons, the heavy industry, the beer and the 'craggy' miners, as they are so often described. What they have in common with the Scottish working class is their knowledge of football.

Back home in Glasgow, 'Man In The Know' of *The Glasgow Observer* chortles in vicarious glee at Newcastle's triumph and singles out young McMenemy for praise by saying that 'he was efficient without having the drive of his father', and remarking on how far he had come in the one year from Scottish junior football to an English Cup medal winner, thus augmenting the already massive total of major medals won by the McMenemy family to 21 (twelve Scottish League medals, eight Scottish Cup medals and one English Cup).

Harry McMenemy's rise owed almost everything to Andy Cunningham. Andy was a Ranger of the old school, clearly well nurtured by Bill Struth, with a commendable lack of tolerance of bad behaviour. He had been instrumental in the departure of Hughie Gallacher, for example, a very unpopular move among the supporters, but he felt that Gallacher's lifestyle was unacceptable to a Calvinistic Scot like himself. By the same token Cunningham saw in the young McMenemy the right attitude, and having played against his father, knew that he was a decent sort of fellow. Harry was given every encouragement, and paid Andy back for his encouragement with effort, commitment and not a little talent.

Andy Cunningham and Jimmy McMenemy, of course, although on different sides of the Celtic/Rangers divide, were men who thought the same way. They had both played for Scotland and were good friends. Jimmy was of course very fond of his youngest son and was delighted to see the progress that he was making. Often, if he had a choice of going to watch Harry or John, he would go to see Harry, for he did not then have the problem of supporting Motherwell while wondering how Celtic were doing. In England, it was straightforward. He was a Newcastle supporter!

Sadly, Harry's career did not really take off as much as it might have after the glories of Wembley. He was injury prone, and the team began to struggle, failing to bring back to Tyneside the glory days of the Edwardian era. In the same way as Celtic sympathisers would sigh and talk about Gallacher, Napoleon and Quinn, Newcastle supporters yearned for the return of Veitch, McWilliam. Higgins and Appleyard. But Harry kept plugging away and found himself chosen to play for Scotland against Wales in October 1933. Sadly he was injured – and his place went to *John* McMenemy. Equally sadly for the McMenemy family, Scotland lost 2–3 and neither Harry nor John were ever again invited to play for Scotland.

Harry continued to play for Newcastle until 1937 then finished his career with a good season with Dundee (under Andy Cunningham again, for he had been sacked by Newcastle). He then returned to Glasgow to live and was frequently seen at Celtic Park until only a short time before his death in 1997.

Another son of Napoleon, Joseph never played professional football, but did have one indirect effect on Celtic. He was on holiday in Ireland sometime in the late 1940s and was walking by

Lough Gill in County Sligo when he saw a girl swimmer apparently in trouble. He dived in and saved her. The grateful girl invited him back to meet her parents and family. Her name was Lily Fallon and she introduced him to her brother Sean. They got round to talking about football, and it was from this conversation that Sean's interest in Celtic began, especially after Joseph sent him a Celtic jersey and a copy of Willie Maley's book *The Story of The Celtic*. Sean signed for Celtic in 1950 and has since then made a huge contribution to the team.

Chapter 9

SCOTLAND

It has sadly become the fashion in recent decades to debunk and scorn Scotland. It may be that the fiasco of Argentina in 1978 or the appalling performance against Costa Rica in 1990 had a longer term effect than what we feared at the time, but the sad fact is that the form of Scotland's International team is now looked upon as a national laughing stock, and we can even detect from time to time, even in the utterances of journalists and pundits, let alone the average punter, a gloating pleasure in the misfortunes of Scotland.

There are many reasons for this dreadful state of affairs, the main one being perhaps the willingness of our top teams to employ mediocre foreign players (one comes to dread every January 'transfer window' for what might suddenly appear!) while shamefully neglecting home grown talent. There is also the undeniable desire of some players to dodge playing for Scotland with 'injuries' which suddenly heal up when their club needs them. All in all, it is a deplorable situation.

It was emphatically not the case in McMenemy's time. On one occasion he 'dodged the column' by choosing to play for Celtic rather than Scotland, but thus was the exception which proved the rule, for it was an unofficial Victory International in April 1919 against Ireland, and he felt justified in turning Scotland down for his colleague Patsy Gallacher had similarly turned Ireland down, or to be strictly accurate, Celtic had refused him permission. McMenemy felt that his refusal to play 'for business reasons' would balance things out. There was also perhaps the additional point that the game was to be played in Belfast, a far from salubrious spot in 1919.

Neither man would have done this if it had been a proper International. Internationals were important things. For a start there were only three per season against Ireland, Wales and England with the game against England (referred to simply as 'the' International) considered to be the highlight of the season, much anticipated with every amateur 'selector' arguing the case in pub, workyard, playground and terracing from New Year onwards and much dissected afterwards with statements like 'if they had only picked..., things would have been so much different'.

Playing for Scotland was an honour. The word 'capped' was used, for every player who played for his country in any season was given a cap with a tassle on it, on which was inscribed the games in which he had played. Normally Scotland were expected to beat Ireland and Wales (although Wales had famously beaten Scotland at Tynecastle in 1906) but the games against England were tight with Scotland looking unlikely ever to emulate their feat of winning five games in a row against England as they had done in the 1880s.

There were also 'League' Internationals for which only players playing currently in a Scottish League team were eligible. They were normally against the English or the 'Football' League played in the country where the 'big' International was not being played, and against the Irish League as well, although from 1904 until 1909, the Scottish League had turned snobbish and considered the Irish League to be 'sub-standard' and not worth playing!

To modern eyes, the organization of the Scotland team seems incredibly amateurish. There was no manager or supremo, and the teams were chosen by Selectors, usually men who were Directors of clubs, and they would serve a few years as Selectors. There were normally seven of them, to make it easier for a vote if required, and the procedure seems to have been as follows. The Chairman says 'Goalkeeper'. Someone would say 'I propose…' Someone else would say 'I propose…' If both men were seconded, they would then move to a vote. They would then move on to right-back and so on.

As we say, appallingly amateurish to modern taste, but before we hasten to condemn, we would do well to recall that Scotland was the best team in the world at that moment, and would be for many years afterwards. Nor did anyone seem to think it odd at the time. Although there would be the odd grumble about one particular Selector being pro-Rangers, or anti-Anglo (ie against players who played for English teams), very seldom was it argued that the system was wrong.

Napoleon wore Scotland's colours on 12 occasions in official Internationals viz.

Ireland	Celtic Park	18/03/1905	4-0
Ireland	Ibrox	15/03/1909	5-0
Wales	Kilmarnock	05/03/1910	1-0
England	Hampden	02/04/1910	2-0
Wales	Cardiff	06/03/1911	1-1
Ireland	Celtic Park	18/03/1911	2-0
England	Goodison	01/04/1911	1-1
Wales	Tynecastle	02/03/1912	1-0
Wales	Celtic Park	28/02/1914	0-0
Ireland	Belfast	14/03/1914	1-1
England	Hampden	04/03/1914	3-1
Ireland	Celtic Park	13/03/1920	3-0

Jimmy's games for Scotland.

He scored five goals – twice against Ireland in 1909 'when the Ibrox stand rose repeatedly to hail the wizardry of McMenemy', once against Ireland in 1911 and his two famous goals at Hampden to beat England in 1910 and 1914. His record of eight wins and four draws is an impressive one. He was never on the losing side.

The strange thing is the four year gap between 1905 and 1909 when he was at the absolute peak of his powers at Celtic Park, orchestrating the success of the team generally agreed to be the greatest of its day, and until 1967, the greatest Celtic team of all. There were of course several reasons for this. The 'conspiracy theorists' of course will tell you that even then there was a strong element of freemasonry in the Scotland selection set-up. That is as may be, but there was another reason as well, and that was Bobby Walker of Hearts who earned nicknames like 'the wizard' for his brilliant play and who was at least the equal of McMenemy, at that time. Indeed a fine piece of play by any other player was even referred to as a 'walkerism' by the journalists of *The Scotsman* in particular. Although Celtic fans would argue for McMenemy, pointing out that in a 'head-to-head' ie when Celtic and Hearts met, McMenemy tended to be on the winning side more often than not, no one could reasonably object to the presence of Walker in a Scotland shirt.

The other thing was that from 1905 until 1909, McMenemy was not absolutely outstanding in the Celtic side. He was simply one brilliant player among many, and although those who really studied the game in detail would come up with the idea that McMenemy was the 'primus inter pares' (a Latin phrase meaning 'the first among equals'), Scotland Selectors did not always see it that way being more impressed by the more flamboyant and obvious skills of Alec Bennett and Jimmy Quinn without appreciating that it was Napoleon who made them tick.

Curiously, all his games for Scotland were at inside-right, even when in the middle of the 1911–12 season he moved to inside-left for Celtic to accommodate Patsy Gallacher. Gallacher was of course Irish and could not play for Scotland in official Internationals, but McMenemy thus found himself in the strange position for this era in which players' positions were far more rigidly defined of playing for Celtic at inside-left, then Scotland at inside-right. He coped admirably with both.

For the Scottish League, McMenemy played 13 times between 1909 until 1920. Once again, they were reluctant to play him before 1909, and the Scottish League bravely kept playing Internationals during the 1914–15 season until political pressure (and perhaps a 1–4 hammering from the English League at Celtic Park in March 1915) put a stop to it. The game that McMenemy played on 5 April 1919 is technically a 'Victory League International'. His record in League Internationals of eight wins, two draws and three defeats is not as good as that in full Internationals, but it is still more than acceptable. He scored twice – once against the Irish League in 1910 and the other against the English League in the Victory League

The 13 Scottish League games Jimmy played in.

Irish League	Firhill	25/10/1909	2-0
English League	Ewood Park	26/02/1910	3-2
Irish League	Belfast	31/10/1910	3-1
English League	Ibrox	04/03/1911	1-1
English League	Ayresome Park	17/02/1912	0-2
English League	Hampden	01/03/1913	4-1
English League	Turf Moor	21/03/1914	3-2
Southern League	Millwall	12/10/1914	1-1
Irish League	Belfast	18/11/1914	2-1
English League	Celtic Park	20/03/1915	1-4
English League	Ibrox	05/04/1919	3-2
Irish League	Belfast	05/11/1919	2-0
English League	Celtic Park	20/03/1920	0-4

International of 1919. Curiously, the two times that he played for the Scottish League at Celtic Park were both heavy defeats, with the game in March 1920 being the last time that he played a representative game.

He also played in the two Victory Internationals against England in 1919. Unfortunately they are not regarded as full Internationals on the grounds that neither country had all their men back from the war, but they were much talked about and looked forward to at the time, and there is a strong argument that they should be given full International status.

| England | Goodison | 26/04/1919 | 2-2 |
| England | Hampden | 03/05/1919 | 3-4 |

The two Victory international games against England.

Quite clearly the highlights of McMenemy's International career were the games against England. On 2 April 1910 106,205 were at Hampden to see what was then regarded as Scotland's best ever triumph over the Auld Enemy.

Scotland: Brownlie (Third Lanark), Law (Rangers) and Hay (Celtic); Aitken (Leicester Fosse), Thomson (Sunderland) and McWilliam (Newcastle United); Bennett (Rangers) McMenemy (Celtic) Quinn (Celtic) Higgins (Newcastle United) and Templeton (Kilmarnock).

England: Hardy (Liverpool), Crompton (Blackburn Rovers) and Pennington (West Bromwich Albion); Ducat (Woolwich Arsenal), Wedlock (Bristol City) and Makepeace (Everton); Bond (Bradford City) Hibbert (Bury) Parkinson (Liverpool) Hardinge (Sheffield Wednesday) and Wall (Manchester United).

Referee: Mr Mason, Burslem

McMenemy was of course at home playing between Bennett and Quinn in the forward line, but this was a magnificent Scottish team in any case, containing men like Newcastle's Peter 'the Great' McWilliam who was good enough to take Jimmy Hay's position, although Jimmy played at left-back. At right-half was Andy 'The Daddler' Aitken and at centre-half Charlie Thomson with whom McMenemy had had many a tussle in his Hearts days.

Hampden looked splendid that day. As McMemeny was well aware it was less than a year since the ground had been damaged (some thought irreparably) in the Hampden Riot. Napoleon had bad memories of that day, although the players were never in any danger, and to him with his naturally calm and sensible disposition it was an excellent example of the demonic power of mob rule. It showed what could happen when a crowd fuelled with alcohol and deluded into believing things that as individuals they would never contemplate, simply lost control and ransacked a football ground.

Hampden, however, much loved of the Glasgow middle classes who supported its owners Queen's Park, had recovered well. The stand had been renovated, the terracings enlarged and of particular interest to society, now ten years into the 20th century, telephone and telegraphic systems to relay the progress and eventual result of the game to the population of London, Newcastle, Manchester, Bristol, Edinburgh and Aberdeen, all gathered outside the offices of their local newspapers and expecting with bated breath the news they had been awaiting for months.

This was the day that McMenemy and Quinn proved themselves to Scotland. They had already proved themselves to Celtic, but had not yet had the opportunity of doing so for the wider population of Scotland. 'Flags and handkerchiefs could be seen waving, whistles were shrilling and bells were ringing' is the picturesque description of *The Glasgow Herald* on the two occasions that Scotland scored, once when Templeton released Quinn with McMenemy alongside him, and 'Jimmy passed to Jimmy' before Napoleon put Scotland one up. Then Quinn, as he frequently did, simply barged defenders out of the way (this was legal at the time) as he ran through to score the second.

England were well defeated long before the final whistle and owed a great deal to their goalkeeper Sam Hardy of Liverpool for keeping the score down to 2–0, and there could be little doubt that the man who orchestrated it all was the formidable Napoleon, who impressed the visiting English journalists by his passing, his control, his turn of speed and his ability to nip out of the way and avoid coarse charges from English defenders.

The following year, Scotland, following a draw against Wales and a win over Ireland, were at Goodison Park, Liverpool, the home of Everton. England as yet lacked a 'home' that Wembley would become in the 1920s, and the games against Scotland were moved about. The largest ground was the Crystal Palace, but Internationals v Scotland had been played at Blackburn, Newcastle, Bramall Lane, Sheffield and other venues.

Liverpool was close enough to Scotland to encourage no fewer than ten special trains to leave St Enoch's Station in the wake of the 'team train' which left immediately before. Indeed, there was a ceremony for a lucky horseshoe, bedecked in tartan and white heather was presented to McMenemy on behalf of the Scottish team before the train pulled out. It was of course a sign of the times (and much deplored by traditionalists) that there were only six players who left from Glasgow – Alex Smith, Alec Bennett and Willie Reid of Rangers, Jimmy McMenemy and Jimmy Hay from Celtic and Donald Colman from Aberdeen. The rest were Anglo-Scots – three from

Newcastle, and the other two from the unlikely sources of Leicester Fosse and Swindon Town. There were also some intrepid Scottish fans who sailed to Merseyside from the Broomielaw to support the team, but the crowd was a poor one of only 38,000 of whom more than half seemed to be Scottish.

The Scottish Selectors had picked the team, but there was some sort of idea that someone had to be in charge of the team, for Clyde's trainer, a man called William Struth, a stern disciplinarian was put in charge to see to it that there was no nonsense involving drink or horseplay. On a previous visit to Liverpool, in 1895, the great Dan Doyle of Celtic, had disappeared. Struth made sure that nothing like this happened, and in later years, of course, he would become the legendary manager of Rangers.

The teams on 1 April 1911 were;

England: Williamson (Middlesbrough), Crompton (Blackburn Rovers) and Pennington (West Bromwich Albion); Warren (Chelsea), Wedlock (Bristol City) and Hunt (Leyton); Simpson (Blackburn Rovers), Stewart (Newcastle United), Webb (West Ham United), Bache (Aston Villa) and Evans (Sheffield United).

Scotland: Lawrence (Newcastle United), Colman (Aberdeen) and Walker (Swindon Town); Aitken (Leicester Fosse), Low (Newcastle United) and Hay (Celtic); Bennett (Rangers), McMenemy (Celtic), Reid (Rangers), Higgins (Newcastle United) and Smith (Rangers).

The referee was Mr William Nunnerley of Wales, and he would be the most talked about man in Scotland for months after this game, for on two occasions (once for definite and once with an element of doubt) the ball seemed to cross the England line but a goal was not given. The first was when McMenemy sent over an inch perfect cross for Sandy Higgins to head goalwards only for the burly frame of England's Bob Crompton to head the ball out when he seemed to be behind the line. That one was doubtful, but the second one was about a yard over the line. Alec Bennett crossed this time, and once again it was Higgins who headed the ball, but then he collided with the post and landed up (injured) in the back of the net. Meanwhile, the ball had also hit the post and seemed to be well over the line before goalkeeper Tim Williamson grabbed it. Mr Nunnerley however said 'No' in spite of heated protests which McMenemy with his 'Keep the Heid, Scotland!' did well to calm down.

This was after a man with the very Scottish sounding name of Jimmy Stewart had scored for England much against the run of play, for virtually the whole ninety minutes had seen Scotland, inspired by McMenemy, pressing and pressing but foundering on the mighty rocks of Bob Crompton and Jesse Pennington. Only four minutes remained when Scotland forced a corner down the left. Alex Smith took it, and he found the head of Sandy Higgins who gave Williamson no chance. In some ways it was McMenemy's best ever International, but it was a disappointment for England's undeserved draw was enough to win the Championship for they had beaten Wales whereas Scotland had drawn in Cardiff.

He was not chosen in 1912 or 1913 in both cases because he was not 100% fit. In 1912 at Hampden, Scotland actually played three centre-forwards in the forward line (with Jimmy Quinn on the left wing) and could only draw 1–1, and in 1913, Scotland simply had a bad day and lost 0–1 at Stamford Bridge. In 1914, however, McMenemy could simply not be ignored (this was the season that he and Patsy Gallacher were inspiring Celtic to a League and Cup Double) and in some ways it was 'his' International. It was certainly not unknown in the next few years, for example, in the Great War as Royal Scots were relieving Sherwood Foresters in the trenches for the odd remark about 'McMenemy' to be made!

The teams were:

Scotland: Brownlie (Third Lanark), McNair (Celtic) and Dodds (Celtic); Gordon (Rangers), Thomson (Sunderland) and Hay (Newcastle United); Donaldson (Bolton Wanderers), McMenemy (Celtic), Reid (Rangers), Croall (Falkirk) and Donnachie (Oldham Athletic).

England: Hardy (Liverpool), Crompton (Blackburn Rovers) and Pennington (West Bromwich Albion); Sturgess (Sheffield United), McCall (Preston North End) and McNeal (West Bromwich Albion); Walden (Tottenham Hotspur), Fleming (Swindon Town), Hampton (Aston Villa), Smith (Bolton Wanderers) and Mosscrop (Burnley).

Referee Mr H. Bamlett, Gateshead.

Hampden on 4 April 1914 was a sight to behold. The attendance was given as 105,000, but climbings over the wall and other illegal methods of entry accounted for more than that, and in any case when the panicky authorities closed the gates half an hour before the start, it was estimated that about 40,000 were still outside, some of whom did not take very kindly to the idea and picked fights with the police. Others, less inclined to violence and more constructive, climbed the huge mound on the north side of the ground and endeavoured to watch the game from there, while still more hoisted each other over the wall when the police were distracted.

It is often said that this was 1914 and people were determined to enjoy themselves while the could before the cataclysm began. This is arrant nonsense, for no one would have guessed what was to happen later that year. Unlike the late 1930s when it was patently and painfully obvious to anyone what was about to unfold, spring 1914 was serene, calm with no greater issue at stake than 'Votes for Women' or the perennial problem of Ireland.

Scotland had three men in the forward line who were less than household names in Alec Donaldson, Jimmy Croall and Joe Donnachie of Bolton, Falkirk and Oldham respectively. They might have been overwhelmed by the sheer vastness of the crowd and the size of the occasion, but McMenemy, once again donning his 'mentor' role as he had done so successfully with Andy McAtee and Patsy Gallacher at Celtic, calmed everyone down and brought out the best in the newcomers.

By half-time, both sides had scored, Charlie Thomson following a corner kick for Scotland, and Harold Fleming following a free-kick for England, but Scotland remained the better team, both McMenemy (twice) and Reid having missed difficult chances 'amidst much groaning from the tartan partisans'.

But soon after the changeover, the tartan partisans had much to cheer about, for McMenemy, having won Scotland a corner kick, managed to shake off his marker and had little problem in banging the ball home from ten yards. Then soon after that, with McMenemy rampant and Scotland dominant, he tried a cheeky chip from outside the penalty area. To his chagrin, the ball hit the bar but rebounded gently for Willie Reid to nudge home. Willie turned immediately to Napoleon to acknowledge his part in it all.

From then on, Scotland were in complete control, and only the brilliance of Sam Hardy in the England goal prevented a massacre, with even the white rosetted English supporters (a good 20,000 of them, it was estimated) applauded the play of McMenemy and asked why on earth he had a nickname like Napoleon? It was a fine Scottish victory, much spoken about and dissected in the dark years that were to follow.

It is a shame on officialdom that the Victory Internationals of 1919 are not recognised, even though caps were awarded, as an auction held in December 2010 in Edinburgh indicated. The argument against their inclusion in official records is that the war was technically still going on until the Peace Treaties were signed in summer 1919, and that neither country was at full strength with so many men still in the forces. In addition, 1919 was not a little chaotic, and there is the well documented story that the Victory International against Ireland saw Scotland begin with only nine men, for Alec McNair and Jimmy McMullen were delayed by chaos on the railway, and the slightly more dubious story that Andy Wilson, a convalescent patient at the Yorkhill Hospital, was on his way to watch one of the games and was still wearing the 'hospital blue' uniform of the war wounded when he was offered a chance to play.

The argument against that was of course the undeniable fact that these games (26 April at Goodison and 3 May at Hampden) were looked upon as nothing other than Scotland v England, much looked forward to and much cherished. The game at Hampden managed to attract 80,000 – something that says a great deal about war casualties when one thinks about the six figure crowds before the war, but there was also the additional problem of a rail strike that day. In the context, 80,000 was a massive crowd. They saw a strange game in which England were 3–0 up, then Scotland pulled two back, then England scored again before Scotland set up a grandstand finish by scoring again, and might even have snatched an equaliser. But 3–4 it was, in a very even game just like the 2–2 draw at Goodison the week before. McMenemy is said to have scored in that game (although sources vary, and there were labour and other problems in the newspaper industry as well as the railway) and he is given a good mention in the Hampden game as well.

There were of course special problems involved for McMenemy and other Celtic players when Scotland were playing Ireland. Yet it is important not to overstate this. Football in Ireland, always more popular in the anglicised, industrialised north of the country, did not really have the sectarian overtones that it would have later in the twentieth century, and the fact that there was a Scottish team in Glasgow founded by Irish immigrants need not necessarily have caused too many problems in Protestant Ulster, even though the same club boasted of having a Roman Catholic cleric in Brother Walfrid among their founding fathers and had had their new ground 'consecrated' in 1892 by the planting of shamrocks by the well known Fenian Michael Davitt.

It cannot be denied however that on the only occasion that McMenemy played for the full Scotland side in Ireland (he played four times against Ireland in Glasgow), the air would have been full of political tension. This was on 14 March 1914 when Ireland seemed to many political observers in mainland Britain to be on the brink of civil war as the Protestant North refused to accept the British idea of Home Rule for Ireland. Their bogus slogan 'Home Rule is Rome Rule', put around by extremists, influenced a great deal of the population, and had not a greater struggle in the shape of the Great War broken out in August, the situation would not have been resolved without a great deal of bloodshed. As it happened, the problem was only postponed.

But there was another issue at stake, and it was the destination of the British International Championship. 31,000 saw a great game on a wet and windy day when Scotland visited Windsor Park, Belfast (it was originally scheduled for Cliftonville but moved to attract a bigger crowd) with Scotland scoring through Joe Donnachie, and seeming to have the game well won until Ireland equalised in the last minute. This goal, scored by Sammy Young of Airdrieonians, was a highly significant goal in the context of Irish footballing history, for as they had already beaten Wales and England, whereas Scotland had drawn with Wales, it meant that Ireland were the British champions for the first time.

In fact the March game was McMenemy's first visit of two to Ireland in the momentous year of 1914, for he returned on 18 November 1914 for a Scottish League game against the Irish League and thus time McMenemy was on the winning side as the Scotsmen won 2–1. By this time of course the country was at war, and eyebrows were raised both in Scotland and Ireland about this game being played. Official Internationals had stopped for the duration, but the League Internationals continued for another season.

The game that McMenemy played for Scotland against Ireland in 1920 was of course a record breaker in that he became the oldest man to play for Scotland and would remain the oldest outfield (ie not a goalkeeper) player to play for Scotland for 90 years. Oddly enough no great deal was made of it in the contemporary press. There was almost the assumption that there was something immortal in Napoleon, and even in season 1920–21 when he was playing for Partick Thistle, there were those who felt that Scotland could do worse than play him.

Wales were the nation who had risen in the Edwardian era. They had some great players, notably Billy Meredith (a man who owed a great deal to Willie Maley's brother, Tom who had managed him at Manchester City), and several men with the very Welsh name of Jones. In the five years before McMenemy was given a game for Scotland, they beat Scotland four times. Having beaten Scotland for the first time ever at Wrexham in 1905, Wales proceeded to get the better of them once again at Tynecastle in 1906 – a result which rocked Scotland who did not believe that such things could happen – then once again in 1907 before Scotland stopped the rot with a 2–1 win at Dens Park in 1908. Wales hit back in 1909 at Wrexham, however, and then at long last McMenemy was given a game against Wales in 1910.

This was a win at Rugby Park, but as far as McMenemy was concerned, it was a decidedly 'Pyrrhic' one, for he was badly injured following a shocking tackle from a Welshman, and missed the Scottish Cup semi-final for Celtic, in which they lost to Clyde. McMenemy was also on the winning side at Tynecastle in 1912. The draw that Scotland earned at Cardiff in 1911 was an honourable and deserved one, but it is generally agreed that the 0–0 draw that he played in at Celtic Park in 1914 was one of the dullest of all time.

McMenemy's heyday was of course long before Scotland played games against foreign opposition and when the World Cup (it would eventually start in 1930) was little more than a twinkle in someone's eye. This is a shame for it would have allowed more of the world to see McMenemy at his best. As it was, the British International Championship was in effect the championship of the world for foreign nations had not yet reached the standard that the British nations had set. But Napoleon was one of the stars of the British Championship, and there is little doubt that he would have graced a world stage as well.

Chapter 10

LEGACY

On 19 October 1957, Celtic won the Scottish League Cup by beating Rangers 7–1, quite clearly one of the best results in their history. Two ex-Celts sat chortling in the stand. One was Davie McLean who had played between 1907 and 1909 and the other was Napoleon. Referee Jack Mowat's full-time whistle brought some relief to Rangers, the League Cup was presented and the players trooped off to their dressing room. McMenemy said to McLean, 'Let's go down and congratulate them!' McLean was more cautious, for he was aware that there were such things as policemen and stewards to be negotiated. 'Never mind that, Davie!' said Napoleon and away he went.

It was a mark of his status in the game that everyone immediately yielded to them. An officious steward was silenced by his superior. 'That's McMenemy' he said, and McMenemy, now nearer 80 than he was 70, and McLean strode on, knocked on the dressing room door, were greeted by McGrory, enjoying one of his rare managerial triumphs, and immediately recognised by great men like Willie Fernie, Bertie Peacock, Bobby Collins, Charlie Tully and the hero of the moment Billy McPhail who had scored a hat-trick. Thus in addition to the greatest footballing experience of their lives, these players, having written their names in Celtic and footballing immortality, could also say that they met Jimmy McMenemy, a man whom even Jimmy McGrory still held in the greatest awe.

Yet, he was just an ordinary man. One day in about 1962, before a game at Parkhead, a few supporters were gathering round the main entrance hoping to see some of the players arrive in their Ford Anglias and Morris Oxfords and Triumph Heralds which were all the rage of the affluent society. Suddenly two elderly men appeared, walking up London Road and made their way through the crowd. Both men were old, but still sprightly and looking fit for their advanced years.

'That's Napoleon!' said fathers to sons as the smaller of the two men, wearing a long, brown coat and soft hat, smiled back. 'Dae ye think we're gaun tae win the day, Jimmy?' asked a bold supporters. Jimmy smiled again 'Well, I hope so' and proceeded into the ground. Youngsters asked 'Who was that?' 'Who was Napoleon?'. Fathers then took deep breaths and told sons who he was. It was so odd that such a great man could have such an ordinary demeanour. He was just a Celtic supporter, like everyone else.

Yet Jimmy would have been distressed in so much that he saw at Parkhead in those days. From 1955 until 1965, there was never a credible challenge mounted for the Scottish League, and to balance the 7–1 League Cup Final win over Rangers, there were four distressing Scottish Cup Final defeats, three of which might have been won in the first game but went to painful replays, and the other in 1956 which saw a curiously lethargic performance against Hearts, about which one feels that the whole truth has yet to be revealed.

Jimmy McMenemy however would appear at Supporters Rallies, receiving a prolonged standing ovation at one in 1962 – he was more or less the only one of Maley's great Edwardian side still alive – and he assured the support that the good days were not far away. He told *The Scottish Daily Express* that 'Celtic will beat Dinamo Zagreb all right' in late 1963 when Celtic were about to play that opposition, and was always ready for a quote and to talk to anyone about his beloved Celtic.

He did live long enough to see Celtic win the Scottish Cup on 24 April 1965 under new Manager Jock Stein. He enjoyed that, but passed away a couple of months later at Robroyston Hospital (his home address was 249 Whitehill Street) at the age of 84 on Wednesday 23 June 1965. He was duly 'fortified by the rites' of the Roman Catholic Church and was buried in the plot beside his wife in Dalbeth Cemetery a few hundred yards away from the ground that he had graced for so long.

He was virtually the last of that great team to pass on, although Davie McLean lived until December 1967. In fact Napoleon had survived some of them by a considerable number of years – Quinn had died in 1945, for example, Gallacher in 1953, Sunny Jim in 1922 and his old friend Alec Bennett in 1940, but the club was well represented at his funeral, and there were still a considerable number of older supporters who still talked in glowing terms about Napoleon. There were also, of course, a great number of players from the team that he coached and nurtured in the 1930s – McGrory and Delaney, for example. It would have been nice if he had lived long enough to see the great triumph at Lisbon in 1967, but he always felt that having survived the Spanish flu of 1918 when his life was reportedly in the balance, that every subsequent year was a bonus.

James E. Handley in his *The Celtic Story* – an occasionally anecdotal and romantic history of the club laced with not a little of the Celtic paranoia, but nevertheless a fine piece of work written by a man who saw the old players, including McMenemy, in the flesh has this quote about Napoleon:

The disgruntled player had a point when he said that in any game in which McMenemy was engaged, two footballs should be allowed – one for McMenemy's private use and the other for the common good. McMenemy was the master of the deceptive movement. His facility for shaking off a cloud of opponents by one simple unexpected turn was unequalled. Nobody excelled him in the art of making an adversary look foolish. He manipulated the ball with the insolent ease of a Harlem Globetrotter and treated the field as a gigantic switchboard, accurately distributing his passes where they were calculated to evoke the best response.

But the greatest thing about him was his humility. He was indeed a man that one could pass in the street. He would be well dressed, dapper and neat, a gentleman who would help ladies to get prams on to the buses and when accosted by a drunk (as used to happen distressingly often even during the day on Glasgow's buses), he would be polite, courteous and dignified. He was a man who had very few enemies – Rangers players and supporters were of course opponents, but they were not foes – and even those who had done him some injustice in the past were very soon reconciled and forgiven.

His manager Willie Maley died in 1958, and the writer of *The Glasgow Herald* amused himself by picking a team of all-time Scotland greats from the mourners. Hardly surprisingly, Napoleon was chosen as inside-right alongside Jimmy McGrory in the centre and Bob McPhail of Rangers at inside-left. What a trio that would have been!

It is of course pointless to argue who was the greatest of them all, for they all lived in different eras and in different circumstances, but it would be hard to deny McMenemy a mention in this mythical contest. Not only was there a tremendous contribution to the club as a player between 1902 and 1920, but there was also his sterling work as trainer, tactician and teacher during the great years of the late 1930s. McMenemy was involved with the club ONLY when they were successful. That must count for a great deal.

STATISTICS

	Scottish League		Scottish Cup		Glasgow Cup		Glasgow Charity Cup		Medals	Scotland Caps	Scottish League Caps	Victory Caps
	Apps	Gls	Apps	Gls	Apps	Gls	Apps	Gls				
1902–03	6	2					3		Glasgow Charity Cup			
1903–04	22	9	6	4	4	1	2		Scottish Cup			
1904–05	15	6	3		3		2	1g	Scottish League Glasgow Cup Glasgow Charity Cup	v Ireland		
1905–06	28	10	3	2	3	1	1	1	Scottish League Glasgow Cup			
1906–07	31	7	9	3	3		2	1	Scottish Cup Scottish League Glasgow Cup			
1907–08	30	7	5	3	4		3	2	Scottish Cup Scottish League Glasgow Cup Glasgow Charity Cup			
1908–09	31	14	6	2	7	4			Scottish League	v Ireland	v Irish League	
1909–10	29	9	3	2	3	3			Scottish League Glasgow Cup	v Wales v England	v English League v Irish League	
1910–11	30	10	6	2	3				Scottish Cup	v Wales v Ireland v England	v English League	
1911–12	21	7	6	3	2	1	3		Scottish Cup Glasgow Charity Cup	v Wales	v English League	
1912–13	23	11	3	2	1						v English League	
1913–14	20	9	6	1	1		2	2	Scottish Cup Scottish League Glasgow Charity Cup	v Wales v Ireland v England	v English League	
1914–15	36	14			1		3	1	Scottish League Glasgow Charity Cup		v Southern League v Irish League v English League	
1915–16	32	9			2		2	1	Scottish League Glasgow Cup Glasgow Charity Cup			
1916–17	34	5			2		2		Scottish League Glasgow Cup Glasgow Charity Cup			
1917–18	24	5			1		2		Glasgow Charity Cup			
1918–19	19	4					1		Scottish League		v English League	v England v England
1919–20	28	2	8	3	3				Glasgow Cup	v Ireland	v Irish League v English League	
With Partick Thistle												
1920–21	29	1	8	1	2		2		Scottish Cup			
1921–22	27	2	3		1							

ND - #0293 - 270225 - C0 - 234/156/12 - PB - 9781780911557 - Gloss Lamination